Contents

iii

Foreword

This year, 2001, marks the tenth anniversary of the Investors in People Standard, which is now widely recognized as the principle national framework that helps organizations succeed and compete through improved people performance.

The 24,259 organizations that have been recognized so far employ between them 5.7 million people – almost 24 per cent of the UK workforce. Fifty of *The Times* Top 100 companies are working with the Standard. A further 3.5 million people are working towards the Standard. This means that in total, at the time of writing, 9 million people are now actively involved and benefiting from Investors in People.

For recognized organizations, the Investors in People Standard has become an accepted and fully-integrated part of working life. Managers up and down the country have understood and embraced the Standard and the positive impact it can have on their businesses. They have recognized that it is not only a mark of best practice for people development, but that Investors in People is a fundamental business tool that informs, impacts and adds value to some of the UK's most successful concerns – be they public or private, voluntary or profit making.

However, it is important to remember that Investors in People accreditation is the **start** of the process not the finish. *Managing for Investors in People* is about continuous improvement: continuing to maintain the Standard and continuing to reap the organizational and business benefits the Standard delivers.

Over the last ten years, the Investors in People Standard has not stood still. It has been revised and updated in direct response to customer feedback. The new version of the Standard, launched last year, is inherently outcomes based, results orientated and flexible, and above all it reflects the changing face of UK business.

This year a recruitment and selection model has also been added to the portfolio. Addressing one of the key issues facing business today, this model enables managers to tie recruitment and selection tightly into long-term business strategy, providing a much-needed tool for identifying and retaining the very best people.

So the Investors in People Standard remains as relevant and appropriate to the workplace of the twenty-first century as it was to the twentieth. Investor in People organizations continue to see the real bottom-line benefits of working with the Standard every day. Over the next ten years, we look forward to more and more managers choosing to gain and, crucially, to maintain the Investors in People Standard.

Ruth Spellman
Chief Executive, Investors in People UK

Introduction

What is Investors in People?

Over the last 10 years Investors in People has become recognized as the major standard for good practice in the development of people to achieve business success. In January 1997 when the first edition of this book was published and just over five years after the first organizations achieved the Standard, over 5,200 organizations have been recognized through the UK. In addition, more than 22,000 organizations were committed to become recognized and actively working towards meeting its requirements. Together these organizations employed about 27 per cent of the UK workforce.

In May 2001 this figure has grown to over 24,250 recognized organizations and another 20,000+ organizations actively working towards meeting its requirements, representing 38.5 per cent of the UK workforce.

It is not just happening in the UK, however. In early 1996 Investors in People was launched in Australia where it is now well established. Investors in People UK is working with partners to establish the Standard in 11 other countries, including for example Holland (where Investors in People (NL) went live in January 2000), Bermuda and Chile, New Zealand, Finland, Germany, Sweden, Malaysia, Jersey, Guernsey and the Isle of Man.

Why read this book?

In our previous books *Investors in People Explained* and *Investors in People Maintained* (Taylor and Thackwray, 2001a, b), we have described what an assessor expects organizations to be able to demonstrate in order to meet the evidence requirements of the Investors in People Standard. In both books we gave an overview of the role played by managers at all levels in helping an organization achieve Investors in People status. It is clear they have a key role in helping organizations achieve recognition and this book is therefore written with a number of purposes in mind:

- To help organizations that are working towards Investors in People and need to gain the commitment of managers to carry out *their* responsibilities for managing the development of people.
- To help managers at all levels to:
  - understand how important their role is in helping organizations achieve and retain Investors in People recognition;
  - be aware of the range of roles and responsibilities that they could be expected to have; and
  - identify whether their own development to date has equipped them to carry out these roles and responsibilities.
- For personnel and training specialists within organizations who are implementing Investors in People.

Who are the managers?

For the purpose of this book, 'manager' means anyone who is responsible for 'managing' the development of people. The term therefore includes everyone from first-line managers (ie, supervisors/team leaders, etc) to the most senior manager in the organization (ie, the Managing Director/Chief Executive, etc). In most industrial sectors these terms will embrace most 'managers'. However, in some sectors different terminology might be used.

What does the book include?

The book further develops a theme outlined in our previous books (Taylor and Thackwray, 2001a, b) – the importance of the role of the manager in achieving Investors in People status. It is based on the practical experience we have gained working with a variety of organizations, all in the Investors in People process from implementation to assessment. Wherever possible it therefore includes illustrations from a variety of named organizations that have either achieved Investors in People status or are currently working towards it.

Chapter 1 sets the scene for the whole book by examining what Investors in People expects organizations to demonstrate. In Part 1, Chapter 2 clarifies who managers are and examines the most common roles and responsibilities that managers have in managing the development of people and how these are changing. It looks at the range of skills and the knowledge and attributes that effective managers need. Chapter 3 then considers what prevents managers from carrying out these roles and responsibilities and what benefits can be gained if they *are* carried out. It also examines what is meant by commitment (to developing people) from the top.

Chapter 4 examines the role of senior managers – who they are, whether they need additional skills and what their role is in achieving Investors in People status for their organizations.

Part 2 opens with Chapter 5, which examines communications. It considers why managers should communicate, what should be communicated and ends by detailing a variety of communications processes we have found in the course of our work as consultants and as Investors in People assessors.

Chapter 6 looks at identifying training and development needs and planning for evaluation. It details a number of approaches to identifying needs and also examines how managers' roles link to the roles and responsibilities of training and development specialists, where they exist. Next, Chapter 7 looks at development that does not involve training and details a number of different approaches, how to plan and structure development.

'Active support' from managers is discussed in Chapter 8. This chapter describes induction processes and examines coaching and feedback skills. Chapter 9 looks at evaluation, what it involves and some approaches that can be taken. The concluding chapter, Chapter 10, examines what managers need to do to help the organization retain Investors in People recognition.

Finally, three appendices include the Investors in People Standard, sources of help available for organizations and a sample evaluation form.

How to use this book

Most chapters are self-contained to enable readers to dip in and out of the book if they wish to do so. However, it is a good idea to read Chapters 1 and 2 first as they set the scene and explain who the managers are. Following the summary at the end of most chapters is a list of the actions required by managers.

CHAPTER 1

Investors in People – The 'Acid Test'

This chapter is essential reading. It sets the scene for the whole book. It examines what is expected from organizations in terms of the required outcomes necessary to achieve Investors in People status. The focus is on what is required from the people within the organization. Subsequent chapters move on to review the implications for managers at all levels.

What is an Investor in People organization?

Many people ask what does the ideal Investor in People organization feel like? In the very early days of the development of Investors in People a number of people involved in the early working groups tried to answer this question. The outcome was a list of statements which they called the 'acid test' for individuals and a list of 'critical success factors' (see Figures 1.1 and 1.2). Using aspects of the above guiding principles, we developed our own set of statements (see Figure 1.3), which we have used when working with organizations.

Looking back at the three sets of guiding principles it is impressive, in spite of three major revisions to the Investors in People Standard, how relevant most of these principles continue to be. Some may

---

The Acid Test

Individuals:

- can accept responsibility to improve continuously;
- can explain their organization's vision;
- can endorse the vision;
- can explain their job and responsibilities;
- can demonstrate competence;
- understand their career options;
- see managers as their coach/supporter.

Figure 1.1 *The acid test*

The Critical Success Factors

- There are committed individuals providing leadership.
- There is a constant valuing of everyone's contribution.
- The strategy/vision/plan is obviously in place.
- Action is constantly taken with regard to culture and attitudes.
- Action is taken on identifying strategic competencies.
- Action is taken on individuals' needs.
- Action is taken on rewards and conditions.
- There is a culture of continuous learning and business improvement.

Figure 1.2 *Critical success factors*

argue with the wording but few would argue with what they are trying to convey.

The key to achieving this type of organization has to be the attitudes and activities of managers at all levels within organizations.

An Investor in People is an organization that:

- has training/development and *learning* in its bloodstream;
- employs people who understand and can explain what the organization is trying to achieve;
- has people who understand how their job contributes to the aims of the business;
- has people who are appropriately skilled and qualified to do the job (or are taking action to develop these skills);
- employs managers who carry out their staff management responsibilities and seek to create a 'learning' environment;
- everyone is committed to continuous improvement and understands what this means in the local context.

Figure 1.3 *An ideal Investor in People*

Outcomes versus processes

One of the key changes in the current Standard[1] concerns the switch in emphasis during the assessment from assessors seeking evidence of processes to seeking evidence of outcomes. Investors in People UK define an outcome as 'the result or effect of an event'.

However, in order to deliver outcomes, processes are generally required. The next section in this book examines some of the processes organizations have used to deliver the outcomes.

The Standard

The Investors in People Standard (see Appendix 1) is broken down into three elements:

- 4 principles;
- 12 indicators;
- 33 mandatory evidence requirements.

To satisfy an assessor that they are an Investor in People, organizations need to demonstrate that they can satisfy each of the 12 indicators. To do this they need to satisfy all 33 of the evidence requirements; 19 of these refer to what is required of the people within the organization.[2] As far as satisfying an assessor, it is these 19 requirements that are the acid test:

- People. . .
  - can consistently explain the aims and objectives of the organization at a level appropriate to their role (indicator 5);
  - can explain how they contribute to achieving the organization's aims and objectives (indicator 7);
  - believe the organization is genuinely committed to supporting their development (indicator 1);
  - confirm that the specific strategies and actions (to support the development of people) described by top management and managers take place and recognize the needs of different groups (indicators 1 and 4);
  - can explain the impact of their development on their performance, and the performance of their team and the organization as a whole (indicator 11);
  - can give examples of relevant and timely improvements that have been made to development activities (indicator 12).

Effective communication of key messages is at the heart of meeting the above requirements; Chapter 5 examines some of the processes organizations have used to communicate effectively.

- People. . .
  - can give examples of how they have been encouraged to improve their own performance (indicator 2);
  - can give examples of how they have been encouraged to improve other people's performance (indicator 2);
  - clearly understand what their development activities should achieve, both for them and for the organization (indicator 6);
  - understand what their manager should be doing to support their development (indicator 8);
  - describe how their contribution to the organization is recognized (indicator 3);

- believe that their contribution to the organization is recognized (indicator 3);
- receive appropriate and constructive feedback on a timely
  and regular basis (indicator 3);
- describe how their managers are effective in supporting their
  development (indicator 8).

While effective communication will contribute to many of the above
requirements, something additional is needed to ensure people are
able to convince an external assessor that the above requirements
are met. A lot of these requirements depend on how people feel
and what they believe. They therefore depend on the right climate
being created by managers and the use of a wide variety of effective
interpersonal skills. Chapter 8 examines some of these issues in
more detail.

- People. . .
  - new to the organization, and those new to a job, can confirm
    that they have received an effective induction (indicator 9);
  - give examples of what they have learnt (knowledge, skills
    and attitude) from development activities (indicator 9);
  - explain the impact of their development on their perform-
    ance, and the performance of their team and the organization
    as a whole (indicator 11);
  - can give examples of relevant and timely improvements that
    have been made to development activities (indicator 12).

Effective communication and the use of effective interpersonal skills
are again required in relation to the above requirements; however,
they also require that the development of people is managed
effectively. This includes planning and evaluating the impact of
development; Chapter 6 looks at these issues in more detail.

Managers, of course, are people too. The assessor will therefore
expect managers, as employees of organizations, to be able to
describe how they feel about the way in which they are communicated with and their development needs identified, addressed and
managed.

Summary

This chapter has described the organizational climate needed to meet the required outcomes of Investors in People. It has explained what is expected from the people within organizations and the types of outcomes required, and has set the scene for the rest of the book, as without action from managers, people are unlikely to describe the required outcomes.

Notes

1. The current version of the Investors in People Standard was launched on 13 April 2000. The basic principles remain unchanged but the Standard is now more focused on outcomes.
2. The list shows 18 evidence requirements as two have been merged under one bullet point.

PART ONE: THE MANAGERS

CHAPTER 2

Who Are the Managers?

This chapter is also essential reading. Again it is part of the scene-setting for the whole book. It examines who the people referred to as 'managers' are and what expectations there are of them. It also examines where the responsibility actually lies for managing people to deliver the outcomes necessary to achieve Investors in People status. It moves on to consider what these responsibilities comprise in most organizations and how they are subject to change. It also examines how they link to the role of training specialists, where they exist within the organization.

The additional responsibilities that senior managers have with regard to managing the development of people are dealt with in Chapter 4.

What is a manager and who is included?

There are many definitions of 'manager'. The *Oxford English Dictionary* defines a manager as: 'a person who is in charge of the affairs of a business etc'. For the purposes of Investors in People, and therefore for this book, the term 'manager' includes *anyone who has responsibility for managing the development of people. It includes everyone from first-line managers to the most senior person within the organization.*

Generally, the term 'manager' can include team leader, supervisor, charge hand, foreman, etc. In some sectors, education for example, there are specific roles identified such as Headteachers, Deans of Faculty, Heads of Schools. Within health, Ward Managers, Sisters, Staff Nurses, General Practitioners and Practice Managers would be included. In organizations such as solicitors' or accountants' practices it includes the partners, although many set up alternative arrangements to manage the development of support staff.

A number of organizations may not have the traditional approach to 'line management'. Structures may be flatter with responsibility devolved or even shared between team leaders. Some organizations operate matrix management where staff may be managed or led by a number of different 'managers' depending on the task on which they are working. Some organizations empower people to make their own decisions about their development. Whatever the arrangements, some person will be responsible for setting the parameters within which individuals can make their decisions. That decision maker will probably be a 'manager' for the purposes of Investors in People.

What are the most common functions of managers?

The broad functions of managers have been established for a long time and, until comparatively recently, have changed very little over the years.

MCI's Management Standards (see Management Charter Initiative, Appendix 2) set the functions of management expected to be performed within an organization. They are frequently used as benchmarks of best management practice. The current Standards describe managers' functions as:

- managing activities;
- managing resources;
- managing people;
- managing information;
- managing energy;
- managing quality;

- managing projects;
- managing environmental performance.

We recently completed a short review of management competencies and found that most of the competencies used by organizations can be traced back to the MCI Standards, although some focused on 'managing for results'.

This book is concerned with managing for Investors in People; therefore we are concentrating on those responsibilities concerned with managing people, in particular the *development* of people.

The responsibilities
The following list of key responsibilities associated with the management of people is drawn from contributions made by participants on a number of management development programmes. They are not presented in any order of priority:

- communicating;
- identifying and agreeing learning, training and development needs;
- planning to meet those needs;
- implementing action to meet the needs;
- coaching/mentoring;
- monitoring;
- resourcing;
- empowering and involving.

The following skills, knowledge and attributes required to manage the development of people were also identified:

- The skills
  - communication skills (eg, questioning, listening, clarifying, presenting, influencing, feedback, counselling);
  - leadership;
  - team building – rapport building;
  - planning/organizing/forecasting;
  - time management;
  - motivating;

- – problem solving – analytical, assessing;
  - – decision-making skills;
  - – coaching/training;
  - – controlling;
  - – delegating.
- Knowledge requirements
  - – the organization;
  - – the jobs;
  - – the people;
  - – the 'rules';
  - – the policies;
  - – the resources.
- Attributes
  - – firmness;
  - – honesty;
  - – enthusiasm;
  - – fairness;
  - – credibility;
  - – consistency;
  - – tact/diplomacy;
  - – being a 'people person'.

This illustrates the vast range of skills and knowledge necessary to be an effective manager of people and, therefore, their development. You may be forgiven, after reading this, for thinking that super-human powers are required! Clearly a manager does not need to be an expert in all these areas, but to be effective, managers need to have a reasonable working knowledge of these skills – and an ability to use them – so that they can be called upon when the need arises.

Surveys of participants on management development programmes asking for information on what training and development they had received to enable them to carry out these responsibilities have for many years revealed a mixed picture, ranging from none to a considerable amount. Significantly, however, the majority of people were at the lower end of the continuum. While the picture is improving, there are still many managers who have had little in the way of training or structured development to help them, particularly in their role of managing people.

Of course there are many more items that could be added to the list of skills and knowledge but we have restricted ourselves to adding just two more: *the management of change* and *project management*. These are of considerable significance as all organizations are living with continual change, both internally and externally. Increased competition, spiralling costs, major policy changes, cuts in funding and a range of other factors conspire to create a fast moving and fast changing environment and managers are at the forefront of these changes and may well bear the brunt of the accompanying pressures. They need to help their people to cope with change and this might well involve managing project teams.

The changing role of managers

Organizations are not alone in being subject to – and causing – change: managers themselves are facing huge changes. Hammer and Champy (1993) describe one essential change as the move from being supervisors to being coaches. This is in line with the recurrent theme in much of the current thinking on the role of people at work, ie, from 'controlled to empowered'.

Two key strategies employed by organizations that impact significantly on the role of managers are delayering and decentralization.

Delayering/flattening structures

Over the last decade by far the most common strategy has involved organizations questioning the need for large numbers of managers at different levels. While this trend has continued (for example, in the first months of 2000 BT announced significant cuts at management level), there is some evidence emerging that is leading some people to question whether delayering may have gone too far. There are many reasons for delayering but two factors stand out as major contributors to the development of the situation.

First, the increased use of technology has made the gathering and utilization of management information a far more refined process. Indeed, the sophistication of the activity is such that in many organizations the view that 'evaluation is the conversion of hindsight into management information' (Peters and Waterman, 1982) is firmly built into everyday working practices.

Second, there is a clearly measurable trend to push more and more responsibility 'down the line'. Regardless of the initial impetus (eg, whether it is driven by the desire to empower people or whether it is cost led) it is on the increase. As people accept this responsibility, several of the functions that formerly comprised part of the manager's role become self-managed by the workforce. Therefore, fewer managers are required. In some organizations whole strata of managers have disappeared as staff have become more empowered. This empowerment means they take responsibilities and, therefore, functions away from the management role.

Decentralizing the personnel and training and development functions

As these layers of management disappeared, a number of organizations have questioned the need for in-house training and development specialists. Many specialist functions can be devolved to managers who themselves have been properly trained and developed. If responsibility is to be transferred as far down the organization as possible, why not do the same with the personnel and training and development functions? In theory, as mentioned earlier, managers have always had training and development responsibilities. Research – and experience – has shown that training and development, such as it was, has been delivered with varying degrees of success. Experience has also shown that the existence of specialists within the organization can lead to some managers abdicating that particular responsibility in practice. Indeed, a similar phenomenon has been observed in some organizations with regard to their Investors in People 'champion'.

Value statements

Finally, another recent trend influencing the role of the manager is the increased and increasing emphasis on the introduction of 'value statements' by organizations. For many years the leading-edge companies have used value statements. For example, since the 1950s Toyota has had an operating philosophy based on a number of values such as:

- the customer always comes first;
- quality applies to everything Toyota does;
- respect for the value of people.

Inevitably when these value statements are introduced they need commitment from managers at all levels to implement them effectively. They also have an impact on management behaviour. This is, of course, especially true when the value statement relates to how people are treated and valued.

The new skill requirements for managers

Managers in the type of organizations described above have a quite different role to the traditional one. To succeed, and be secure, modern managers have to be seen to be 'adding value'. They need to help to integrate quality, to be innovative and, as mentioned above, to manage change. This new role also involves facilitating and supporting their people rather than policing and controlling them. Contemporary managers will be responsible for encouraging and empowering their people to manage themselves within a broad framework. Employees are encouraged to seek improvements through innovation and challenging the status quo. Many managers find this uncomfortable. It may seem ironic, but as employees are empowered many managers need considerable support and encouragement from their own manager in order to develop and practise these new skills and attitudes.

The role of training and development specialists

Where organizations do retain training and development specialists, it is necessary to avoid managers being tempted to abdicate their responsibility for training and development. Therefore, it is important to clearly state what the responsibilities of managers actually are and how they then link to those of the training specialist. Most organizations would simply say that managers are responsible for ensuring that their people have the skills and knowledge to carry out their role. The specialist is responsible for *supporting* managers in fulfilling their responsibilities.

Where specialists do not exist in organizations, managers will need to ensure that training does take place. However, they do not have to deliver the training. People to whom they have delegated appropriate responsibility often carry out the training.

Of course, nominated employees should themselves be trained to carry out these additional responsibilities, although our experience suggests that this is often not the case.

In Chapter 4 we discuss the additional responsibilities that senior managers have for the development of people.

The relevant Investors in People indicators

Of the 33 evidence requirements, there are four that specifically mention managers:

- Managers. . .
  - can describe specific actions that they have taken and are currently taking to support the development of people (in order to improve the organization's performance) (indicator 1);
  - can describe specific actions that they have taken and are currently taking to ensure equality of opportunity in the development of people (indicator 4);
  - at all levels understand what they need to do to support the development of people (indicator 8);

- at all levels can give examples of actions that they have taken and are currently taking to support the development of people (indicator 8).

So managers, as well as describing what their managers do for them, will be expected to describe what they do to support the development of their people.

Summary

This chapter has reviewed the roles and responsibilities of managers relating to the development of people. It has considered what skills, knowledge and attributes managers require to fulfil these responsibilities.

CHAPTER 3

The Manager's Role in Creating a People Development Culture

This chapter examines the barriers preventing managers from carrying out the roles and responsibilities identified in Chapter 2 and how some may be overcome. It considers how commitment – or lack of it – from senior managers can affect their role. It briefly explores issues that prevent the establishment of a culture that encourages people development. It also examines the benefits managers can gain if they do manage the development of their people.

What are the barriers?

The most obvious and commonly quoted reason for not managing the development of people is lack of time and/or pressure of work. Clearly the pressures on the contemporary manager are much greater today than they were some years ago, especially as there are often less of them! However, did managers actually spend any more time developing people 20 years ago than they do now?

That is not to say that training did not take place. The training and development of people has historically been moving towards centre stage since the rise of the Mechanics Institutes during the first part of the 19th century. At one time, in fact, training and development was done in secret – if you were found out you would face the sack and if you organized the training there were possible legal penalties!

Other reasons often quoted for not developing staff are:

- 'Top management merely pay lip service to training and development.'
- 'It's not my job – it's the training department's job.'
- 'If I train my staff too well I'll lose them.'
- 'Developed staff are more challenging/threatening.'
- Lack of resources, especially money.
- Lack of support or encouragement from their line manager.
- Lack of confidence or understanding.
- Overcomplicated or unnecessary systems.
- 'It's not the way things are done round here.'
- Failure to see/understand the benefits.
- Lack of training and development.

Lack of commitment from the top to training and development

The first indicator in the Investors in People Standard is: 'The organization is committed to supporting the development of its people.'

This commitment starts from the top and without it it is more difficult for managers to carry out their responsibilities. If managers themselves are publicly questioning this commitment then that organization will not satisfy an assessor and will not, therefore, be recognized as an Investor in People.

We, as assessors and advisers ourselves, have experienced this situation in many organizations. This occurs mainly in those organizations that are working towards recognition but occasionally in those that have applied to be assessed and believe they meet all that is required by the Investors in People Standard.

It is evident that a number of senior managers feel that all they have to do to demonstrate commitment to developing people is to make a statement such as 'People are our greatest asset.' They then do very little else to convince their people to believe that this is true.

In those organizations where senior managers have always been committed to training and development, this statement may be unnecessary or may have already been made in a variety of locally meaningful ways. For those organizations where it has not been evident that this commitment exists, there is a need to change culture/custom/practice to demonstrate to all staff that investing in people is real and is valued as good practice by the organization.

All managers have a significant role to play here but it is ridiculous to expect managers to reinforce this commitment with their people if they are not convinced themselves. Clearly, therefore, the process needs to begin by convincing the managers and creating the 'climate' for training and development to take place.

There is no one simple answer: the message must be constantly reinforced by action. Senior managers in organizations that have been recognized do a variety of things that demonstrate this commitment, a theme also picked up in Chapter 4.

Lack of encouragement and recognition

As indicated in Chapter 1, the Standard also requires that people feel they have been encouraged to develop and that their contribution is recognized. This too relies on managers creating the right climate, but it is very difficult to build this environment if managers themselves feel neither encouraged nor appreciated. So this again starts at the top of the organization with senior managers encouraging managers to develop in appropriate and relevant ways as well as encouraging them in turn to encourage their people to develop.

Creating a climate where people feel 'recognized' is often much more difficult to achieve. When people are asked about communication they inevitably say it could be better. Similarly when asked if they feel their contribution is recognized they frequently say 'It would be nice to have more recognition.'

The Standard does not require organizations to have a strategy on recognition but it is such a difficult issue to get right that having a strategy would be helpful.

Equality of opportunity for development

The Standard also requires that opportunities to access job-related development are available equitably. As assessors and advisers, we often hear comments such as:

- 'It's ok if you work on the shop floor.'
- 'They're only committed to training technicians.'
- 'If you're in admin you're a second-class citizen.'

Equality of opportunity *for development* means that managers at all levels within organizations should ensure that they have a strategy that ensures that everyone, regardless of function, working hours or location is included in communications processes and has access to the development they need to carry out their role.

Clearly if the amount of training and development needed is huge it will have to be prioritized in line with key business objectives. Those whose needs do not fall into the top priority must understand this to avoid a feeling of inequality of opportunity or comments such as, 'Yes, we have a process for identifying training needs but nothing ever happens.'

In extreme cases, managers themselves may not have equality of opportunity for development. We have seen some organizations where senior managers are not convinced about the merits of management training and development and expect their managers to pick up appropriate skills 'on the job'.

Whatever the situation, senior managers and managers alike need to be convinced about the benefits of people development.

Equal opportunity in this context does *not* mean that all staff should have the same amount of training and development opportunities. The distribution must be in line with job role and/or wider organizational objectives. It is also important to note that equality for all employees will focus on people who are 'remote' from the core business for a variety of reasons, for example:

- what they do (ie, removed from the core business of the organization and therefore find it more difficult to see the links);
- where they are located (ie, geographically remote);
- the nature of their contract (ie, part-time, fixed-term, etc);
- the hours they are at work (ie, evenings, nights, weekends, part-time).

So what's in it for managers?

In many organizations, including a number that we have worked with, it is clear that there is a commitment from the top, yet some managers still do not manage the development of their people effectively.

The managers who ask the question, 'What's in it for me?' are usually those managers who are totally focused on getting the job done. They are often referred to as 'task managers'. Task managers exist in all organizations and at all levels, including the senior team.

Clearly every manager is there to ensure the task is completed: if the job is not done the organization may cease to exist. However, task managers concentrate on getting the job done to such an extent that they often ignore the needs of their people. They are likely to be experts in the task but not at 'managing'. They may well have learnt to manage by observing other 'task managers' and, either by choice or lack of opportunity, have had little training in management techniques. They are not good listeners, they probably believe no one can do the job as well as they can, and if there are problems they will say things such as, 'Leave it to me, I'll sort it out' or, 'Why do I have to do everything myself?' They tend not to trust their staff so delegate very little and invariably they work extremely hard – *because* they do almost everything themselves, sometimes even routine tasks.

Convincing these managers that training and developing their people has benefits is very difficult. Probably having had little training themselves, they wonder why other people should need it. The benefits to these managers of investing in their people are potentially huge.

Time savings

If they *invest* time with their people in training and developing, through sharing their expertise with them, they will find problems don't occur as often because people have been shown how to anticipate them. When they do occur, unless it is a new or critical problem they will be able to deal with it themselves because they will have learnt how to handle it. This releases the pressure and allows the manager to devote more time to dealing with the really critical issues.

The chief danger associated with a task manager is that people become demotivated and mistakes are more likely to occur. People know that their manager will always 'sort things out' if things go wrong. Others may feel that there is little point in showing initiative because things usually go wrong when they do. This may well be the case because they don't fully understand the impact of their actions as it has never been discussed with them.

So, for the task manager the biggest benefit from training and developing staff is likely to be more time – and therefore resource availability – in the longer term.

Job satisfaction

There is a lot of satisfaction to be gained from developing people. It is possible that developed people will move on to better jobs but in the shorter term the manager who develops people will have benefited in a variety of ways from, for example, having taken someone with few skills and little knowledge and helped their development by passing on their own expertise.

Contented staff – reduced turnover

People who have been developed – and are aware that they have been developed – usually appreciate it. They are usually very committed to doing a good job and often stay longer in the job because they get a great deal of satisfaction. If they do decide they need to move on to a more 'stretching' job the manager can derive satisfaction from knowing they have played a key role in helping the person develop and can look forward to starting again with a new person. 'People managers' naturally feel this satisfaction; although they probably feel some regrets about losing a good member of staff they will still take pride in having done a good job as a people manager. 'Task managers' will probably feel that if they hadn't developed them so well the person may not have left. However, this statement clearly suggests that if you don't train staff they'll stay! Research shows that, especially with new starters, the most commonly cited reason for leaving is *lack of adequate* training. This does not always mean they have not had any training but that the training was not felt to be good enough.

Indeed, some organizations place a very high premium on training and development, especially at the initial induction stage. One example is Hewlett Packard, which has an intensive induction over several weeks and underpins its commitment to developing its people with the view that it is 'better to have excellence for a short time than mediocrity for a lifetime'.

Managers who have high staff turnover (or absenteeism) in their teams will find the investment in training and development will pay off quite quickly. Huge savings in time spent on the initial training can be made if they have a more stable team.

Overcoming the 'lack of time' barrier

If you believe in the benefits you will overcome the barriers and make time! This is easy to say but it is true.

Managers who are convinced that the investment in time will pay off find the time even if it means a lot of extra effort in the short term. They will also find the resources. If they are not getting the support from their own manager they will make the case in order to get that support. If the case is well made it would be a very unreasonable manager who failed to support it, especially if they are committed to the value of training and development themselves!

Frequently a lack of time problem is made worse by systems being too complicated or unnecessary. In organizations that are committed to training and developing their people, we have found that the 'culture' encourages the need for complicated systems to be challenged. If they are essential it will be explained why and, even though it may not help time problems, at least people understand the rationale. But if they are not essential then they quite often are changed or scrapped altogether. The myth of bureaucracy being associated with Investors in People is just not true.

Training and development for managers

We have already looked at the skills and knowledge required by managers to effectively manage the development of their people.

Quite often management training courses are filled by people who have these skills and knowledge and are quite capable of managing their people but are looking for additional skills and ideas. Experience has shown that the managers who lack some of these skills and knowledge and really need management training and development rarely volunteer for it. The onus therefore is on senior managers to identify the training and development needs of their managers and ensure that they are met. This does not always mean that they should attend a lot of training courses, but merely that they may require coaching and development on the job.

Managers do not have to be expert trainers and developers, but they must have a broad understanding of some of the basic principles. They should understand the principles of coaching. An outline has been included in Chapter 7.

The relevant Investors in People indicators

In addition to the evidence requirements affecting 'people' outlined in Chapter 1, the evidence requirements indicated at the end of Chapter 2 are also relevant to the issues raised in this chapter:

- Managers. . .
  - can describe specific actions that they have taken and are currently taking to support the development of people (in order to improve the organization's performance) (indicator 1);
  - can describe specific actions that they have taken and are currently taking to ensure equality of opportunity in the development of people (indicator 4);
  - at all levels understand what they need to do to support the development of people (indicator 8);
  - at all levels can give examples of actions that they have taken and are currently taking to support the development of people (indicator 8).

Summary

This chapter has looked at reasons why managers do not always effectively manage the development of their people. It has looked at the need for top level commitment to training and development and what prevents it developing. It has examined the benefits to managers of training and developing their people. Finally, it has made some suggestions that may overcome the remaining barriers that prevent managers carrying out their responsibilities.

CHAPTER 4

The Role of Senior Managers

This chapter develops a number of the issues identified in earlier chapters by looking at the responsibilities of senior managers in managing the development of people.

Who are senior managers?

Most organizations have a team of managers who are considered to be the Senior Management Team. Where the line is drawn between managers and senior managers will vary from one organization to another. For the purposes of this book they are the team that sets strategies and policies and manages (or directs) the managers of the organization.

The responsibilities of senior managers

The key purpose of senior managers has been described by MCI as: 'to develop and implement strategies to further the organization's mission'. It goes on to describe the key issues for senior managers as:

- understanding and influencing the environment;
- setting the strategy and gaining commitment;
- planning, implementing and monitoring;
- evaluating and improving performance.

They also have a responsibility to manage the development of the people who report directly to them but they also set the strategies and policies for *all* people in the organization.

The Cabinet Office has recently piloted a new competency framework for senior civil servants which further develops the above issues and focuses on 'leadership for results':

- giving purpose and direction;
- thinking strategically;
- learning and improving;
- focusing on delivery;
- getting the best from people;
- making a personal impact.

The skills, knowledge and attributes required of senior managers

Chapter 2 of this book describes what managers identified as the skills, knowledge and attributes that they need to manage the development of their people. A close examination of the above responsibilities should reveal that, *to manage the development of their people,* senior managers require, in the main, the same skills and attributes although, as they set the rules, policies, etc for organizations, the knowledge requirements may be different.

They clearly need to have strategic skills, which in terms of developing people will embrace such things as succession planning, management development and other global people issues.

They need to agree policies on induction, qualifications and management responsibilities for the development of people. While these may have been the responsibility of the Personnel Manager in some organizations, the responsibility for personnel matters is being devolved and personnel specialists are themselves either disappearing or taking on additional responsibilities. This leads to senior managers requiring a range of new skills and knowledge.

We feel, based on feedback gained through interviewing employees at all levels in organizations, that a large proportion of senior managers are not as effective in managing the development of people as they should be. They tend to assume that middle managers are quite capable of managing their own development and while this should be true to some extent, middle managers in many organizations are being asked to do a great deal more than they have ever done before and need lots of support from their managers. However, middle managers in many organizations are an endangered species and are therefore unlikely to seek too much support as it may be seen as a sign of weakness.

Commitment to training and development from the top

Perhaps, owing to the various pressures that face them, there is a tendency for many senior managers to be 'task managers' rather than 'people managers' and therefore to overlook the development needs of their people. This also leads to a possible conclusion that they are unlikely to be as committed to developing people as they should be. Alternatively, they consider themselves committed but their actions undermine their commitment because everything they do and say reinforces their commitment, to the task, rather than the people.

Chapter 3 examined how the absence of commitment to training and development from the senior managers can form a barrier, or a ready-made excuse, to the commitment of middle managers. As well as undermining their commitment, it may also affect the development of middle managers.

Even when senior managers *are* committed to training and development, it can be undermined by previous 'initiatives' that they have been committed to. This often results in comments such as, 'I've heard it all before' or, 'I am sure they are committed, but nothing ever happens' from managers and their people. Initiative overload seems to be quite common in many organizations at the moment. The outcome is that many initiatives are not seen through to the end and people become very cynical about the next 'initiative' or 'flavour of the month'.

So what do senior managers need to do to demonstrate their commitment? First they need to develop the strategy to support the commitment to develop people in order to develop the organization. The following chapters will expand on the detail of what such a strategy may contain; however, a key issue inevitably will be communication.

Senior managers being visible and communicating key messages is clearly important but in very large organizations this is not easy. A number of recognized large organizations have produced videos to get these messages across but nothing beats being seen in person. For many years Tom Peters has promoted 'managing by walking about'; this is an extension of the same idea. Again it is not easy in large organizations but they generally have a large top team so it can be shared out between them.

However, being visible and communicating is only part of the process. If nothing happens as a result then people will still not be convinced, so the next stage in demonstrating commitment is to ensure that meeting training and development needs is adequately resourced.

It is quite common to hear comments such as 'Top management are committed until they have to put their hands in their pockets.' Managers and their people will finally be convinced when identified training and development actually takes place.

Finally, they need to ensure that the required people development takes place. Again, in large organizations this is not easy and they, in turn, will need to rely on their managers to demonstrate their own commitment by managing the implementation of development plans. Linking it to the process of evaluating development may enable senior managers to achieve two outcomes for one action. For example, asking managers to report on people development issues and the resulting benefits will enable them to assess that the development has been delivered while at the same time gathering information about its benefits.

Evaluation at senior manager/organizational level

The Investors in People Standard specifically requires top management to be aware of the costs and benefits of developing their people. This means that they should to some extent be involved in, or at least aware of, the evaluation of training at the organizational level. This means that learning, training and development should feature on the agenda of meetings of the Senior Management Team. This should not be a standing item to which mere lip service is paid. Rather it should be planned to take place at certain times of the planning cycle – for example: setting of objectives and learning and development needs; reviewing of achievements; special projects and so on. It is essential that the 'difference' between management and development is minimized as much as possible at this level so as to cascade the 'right' messages down the line.

However, as we have pointed out elsewhere (Taylor and Thackwray, 2001a), evaluation starts at the planning stage. As part of that process senior managers should consider the broad training and development needed to achieve the business plan, especially where there are significant changes being introduced. This should at least include plans to cover health and safety and other relevant legislation; management development strategies; the introduction or expansion of IT and related training. In many organizations it will include looking at aspects associated with quality and customer care that inevitably affect everybody there.

By asking managers to report on development activities periodically, as indicated above, they will ensure that they are aware in broad terms of the impact that it is having on the organization's performance, and enable them to take a view of the overall benefits gained and whether they have received value for money for the resources allocated. In larger organizations this inevitably means having some process, ideally simple, practical and non-bureaucratic, for collating information gathered through management channels.

The relevant Investors in People indicators

Of course many aspects that were discussed in Chapter 1 in relation to how people feel apply equally to senior managers. The requirements for managers highlighted in Chapters 2 and 3 also apply to senior managers, arguably to a greater extent. There are five requirements of the organization and three of top management that quite clearly would be followed up in some detail with senior managers by an Investors in People assessor:

- The organization needs to demonstrate that it:
  - has a plan with clear aims and objectives (indicator 5);
  - has clear priorities that link the development of people to its aims and objectives at organization, team and individual level (indicator 6);
  - makes sure that managers have the knowledge and skills they need to develop their people (indicator 8);
  - can show that people learn and develop effectively (indicator 9);
  - can show that the development of people has improved the performance of the organization, teams and individuals (indicator 10).
- Top management. . .
  - can describe strategies that they have put in place to support the development of people in order to improve the organization's performance (indicator 1);
  - can describe strategies that they have put in place to ensure equality of opportunity in the development of people (indicator 4);
  - understands the overall costs and benefits of the development of people and its impact on performance (indicator 11).

In addition there is a requirement that should be considered by senior managers when developing the strategy to support the development of people:

- development is linked to relevant external qualifications or standards (or both), where appropriate (indicator 9).

Finally where representative groups such as trade unions, works councils, etc exist, senior managers will need to take a view about communications with such groups that impacts on the following evidence requirement: representative groups are consulted about the organization's aims and objectives (indicator 5).

What senior managers need to do

To reinforce their commitment, whenever possible senior managers should:

- be visible and show that they are committed to staff development in both formal and informal discussions with staff;
- ensure that there are adequate resources in terms of time, people and money to meet those development needs that have been identified;
- take every opportunity to recognize and reinforce the valuable contribution people at all levels make to business success;
- ensure all people understand that there are developmental opportunities available that contribute to the development of skills or knowledge needed to meet business requirements;
- ensure that 'initiatives' are seen through to the end;
- tackle those middle managers who are *not* committed.

They need to:

- develop a strategy to support the development of people linked to the needs of the organization;
- plan and agree policies at an organizational level that consider the broad developmental needs required to achieve the business objectives;
- as part of monitoring business performance, review progress of the broad impact of the planned developmental activity, including the roles and responsibilities of managers;
- continually reinforce the contribution development makes to business success;
- celebrate the success of development activity;
- periodically restate their commitment to continue to develop people because it pays to do so.

Summary

This chapter has reviewed the responsibilities of senior managers in organizations who are working towards Investors in People status or maintaining their existing recognition. It has examined the requirements in terms of additional skills and knowledge and outlined what they should actually do to reinforce their commitment to the process at organization, team and individual level.

CHAPTER 5

Communication

This and subsequent chapters develop a number of issues raised in the previous section and examine some of the processes available to deliver the required outcomes. This chapter concentrates on communications – a theme that runs through all aspects of Investors in People. It considers what the manager needs to do to deliver required outcomes associated with effective communication, and outlines some methods of communication used by organizations, the manager's role as a communicator and how this links to the commitment to develop people.

Why communicate?

We have found that no matter how good (or bad) communications are in organizations, people will invariably say they could be better. In that case, why bother?

Research has shown that the most effective organizations are the ones that communicate with their employees on a regular basis. The theory, borne out by research, is that if people understand what the organization is trying to do and how they can contribute to its success, they will generally be more committed and therefore be more motivated to want to help the organization succeed. In a seminar at the IPD Conference in Harrogate in 1998, Ricardo

Semler, author of the best selling book *Maverick,* said, 'the single hardest thing to do is to make people interested in coming to work on Monday morning'. We believe that effective and open communication contributes greatly to overcoming this difficulty.

There are, of course, people who have no wish to be well informed. It would be naive to believe that it is possible to gain the wholehearted commitment of everyone who works for the organization. A large number of people are quite happy to go to work, do their job and go home. They believe they can tell how well the company is doing by the 'orders that are going out of the door' in private sector companies or how well they performed in external audits in public sector organizations. They are not really interested in what's happening in any part of the company but their own. They have never been communicated with in the past so why should they bother listening now? They may well be suspicious of the motives of management who suddenly decide to adopt a more 'open' approach to communication.

There are not many employees who genuinely fall into this category, and their numbers are diminishing. The typical stereotype of this category is the long-serving worker in a traditional industry. When organizations decide to commit to Investors in People, however, it is these people who may cause their managers a significant amount of local difficulty.

What are the key messages to communicate?

We have found that significant numbers of people do appreciate the fact that communications are improving and senior managers are disclosing more about how well the organization is doing and what the future plans are. Of course there will be cases where future plans may not be entirely in keeping with what employees want, but clearly they are better being informed than kept in the dark or misinformed by rumour and speculation.

Today most organizations have vision statements, mission statements and, increasingly, value statements. Ideally these should have been developed in consultation with the workforce. In practice they are often developed by senior managers or in some organizations through events involving all managers. In such situations, it is essential that the meaning and purpose of such statements are communicated effectively to all employees. If they are not communicated, why have them?

We have discovered that a number of organizations communicate their statements through impressive launches and do little else. To get employees to understand and to 'own' the messages in the statements it is important that they are continually reinforced. This means that every message should either directly or indirectly include aspects of the vision, mission or values. As any marketing specialist will tell you, 'it is not the weight of the water that wears away the stone, it is the drip, drip, drip. . .'.

Effective communication should ensure that all people understand how they contribute to the success of the organization, and reinforce senior managers' commitment to developing people by encouraging them to take up development opportunities and ensuring they understand how staff development has contributed – and will continue to contribute – to success at the individual, team and organization levels.

Setting the context for training and development

Another important reason for communicating the future plans of the organization is that it sets the context for development actions. One of the main benefits expressed by organizations who have been recognized as Investors in People is the added focus it has given them in terms of setting business objectives and relating learning and development to them. It has ensured that learning, training and development activity is understood at all levels to be relevant to the needs of the organization. In some organizations it has reduced expenditure on training and development when it is discovered that some elements of the activity were not in line with the organization's objectives. In other words, Investors in People can contribute to a more precise targeting of funding, rather than a scattergun approach.

To enable individuals and their managers to relate training and development to the organization's needs, these needs have to be communicated in the first place. Figure 5.1 illustrates how this works in a large number of organizations. The model has been simplified to show the communication process once organizations

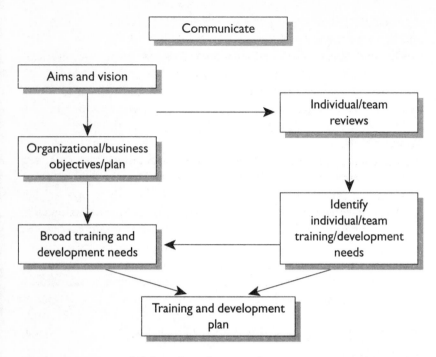

Figure 5.1 *A model for identifying and communicating business and training and development needs*

have clarified their broad aims and vision. This has, in turn, enabled them to devise objectives, usually as part of a plan. This is then communicated to enable the people and their managers to agree relevant training and/or development actions. Then a training and development plan can be drawn up at the organizational level.

Communication processes also present the chance to ensure people are aware of other developmental opportunities open to them, such as seeking external qualifications or engaging in other developmental activities such as conferences, exhibitions, networking, shadowing, 'sitting by Nellie', helping choose/purchase new equipment, etc.

What methods of communication are there?

In very small, single-site organizations, communications should not be a problem, at least in theory, as people constantly work closely together. The senior manager/management is probably very visible and the opportunity to communicate is constantly available. Clearly this is not the case in larger organizations or those that are geographically dispersed. These organizations need to either be more structured in their communications processes or, in some cases, more imaginative.

Team briefings
An increasing number of organizations, especially large ones, are using a formal team briefing process as the method of passing messages to the workforce.

The process will normally involve passing on information, usually on a monthly basis. The information will outline current achievements against the plan and what the next month's targets may be. In addition, senior managers will normally agree what key messages need to be passed on to the workforce; these form the 'core brief'. These may include an outline of future plans and strategies, adjustments to plans, market influences, etc. Team briefs often include information about the people, eg, leavers, retirements and new starters.

The message in the core brief can be passed on unaltered to all employees but managers may wish to add a 'local flavour' as the message is cascaded down throughout the organization. This cascade process normally starts with a member of the senior team briefing the presenters, who will have been trained for this role. In many organizations these 'team briefers' are managers, but this does not always have to be the case. To ensure that everyone gets the message, a transcript of the brief is normally made available so that absentees can read it.

With the growth of new technology, such as networked computer systems, e-mail and intranets, more and more organizations are able to circulate copies of the briefs electronically. This offers the potential to make the process more interactive and to avoid the accusation that 'there is too much information, not enough communication'. Team briefing systems will normally encourage employees to use the system to ask questions and pass messages and concerns back up to senior management.

Advantages of team briefings include:

- consistent messages being passed on to all the workforce;
- the formality of the system ensuring that the process works and happens on a regular basis;
- possibilities for integration into team meetings where they exist.

Disadvantages include:

- as team briefings permeate an organization they might get longer and longer as the local flavour is added if managers find it difficult or are frightened to précis the brief and make it 'bespoke' for their people;
- not presenting information about the organization's performance in simple terms; this is invariably off-putting to most of the recipients;
- the system does not lend itself to certain types of organizations, eg those employing large numbers of part-time workers or job-sharers, continuous process operations, shift working or geographically dispersed organizations, where the challenges of getting everyone together at the same time are almost insurmountable;
- excessive reliance on the quality of the presentation of the 'briefer'. In practice, a large number of organizations do not get as many messages passed back up through the system as they would like.

However, we have found really effective team briefing processes. These occur when briefers have been well trained and are able to facilitate discussion that enables employees to interpret how 'core' messages are likely to impact on their roles.

Regular team meetings, notice boards, etc

Given that the idea of team meetings is hardly a new one, it is surprising how many organizations have not used them or have allowed them to fall into disuse.

Team meetings may not be as formal as team briefings. This can be both an advantage and a disadvantage. The informality can enable a meeting to be called at short notice while an issue is current, but lack of structure can also allow such gatherings to run out of steam.

The most effective team meetings are those that are held on a regular basis, perhaps on a fixed date each month, with short but relevant agendas, some of which may have been set by the team itself.

Although many organizations have used notice boards for years, we have found that their use in some organizations has been viewed as quite radical. They should not be seen as *the* method of communicating but as a supplement to other methods. It is, of course, difficult to check whether messages are getting through if notice boards are the sole means of communicating with the workforce.

Newsletters, in-house journals, memos, etc

These present ideal vehicles for getting messages across in organizations that are geographically dispersed, where the workforce is out-stationed or working from home. Again, there is nothing new about these processes but it is amazing how many organizations do not use them at all or don't use them to communicate key messages.

Newsletters or journals do not always need to be costly, full-colour, printed publications. Provided the message is well presented in clear, easily understood language, most people will take an interest and read them. They can, however, easily be ignored or, as we found out in one organization with a number of locations, be left in a corner, not distributed by unimpressed managers.

Some organizations have used, with great effect, pay-packets or envelopes for sending out pay statements as a means of getting messages to employees, especially those based at isolated and remote locations.

E-mail

Increasingly e-mail (and/or intranets) is being used to circulate messages and we have seen organizations that use the process very effectively. It is clearly cheap and quick, especially in organizations that are geographically spread out or with staff who are employed from home or 'on the road'. It is also very easy to send messages, some of which may be quite long. However, it is the ease with which it can be used that causes some of the problems. Recent research carried out by the Institute of Management and UMIST

(2001) found that 82 per cent of managers surveyed found that the information they handle has greatly increased over the last three years; 54 per cent claimed to suffer from information overload. The use of e-mail must be a contributory factor. People often get deluged with information and sometimes important messages get lost. To avoid this problem many organizations have set up protocols that outline the rules for the use of e-mail. Typically these protocols would set out policy and procedures such as:

- keeping e-mails short and to the point;
- using headings effectively to enable potential readers to decide whether the messsage is relevant to them;
- only marking as urgent or high priority those messages that *are* urgent;
- questioning whether e-mail is the right medium;
- considering carefully who the message(s) need to be copied to;
- encouraging staff to set aside 'e-mail reading times' to avoid being constantly interrupted by the arrival of e-mails.

They will periodically evaluate the use of e-mail and some organizations have started to have 'e-mail-free days'.

Video conferencing
The use of video conferencing appears to be increasing. This again is particularly useful when locations are geographically spread out as it enables people who would be unable to attend meetings to be kept informed and to contribute to discussions.

Videos
This method can obviously be costly but a number of organizations have chosen to use it to get the message across. It offers a chance for senior management in extremely large organizations to be seen and, critically, to be seen to be putting the message across personally.

One particular organization found that the in-house journal was not getting to the people, so the senior management decided to produce a monthly video to put across key messages. To ensure that it was effective and that all the workforce saw it, they trained their managers to 'present' it during monthly meetings. Feedback was sought and subsequently acted upon. One set of feedback led to the message in the video and the language used being simplified, but the overriding message from 'the viewers' was that the video was appreciated.

Company events, conferences, etc

A number of organizations use annual events to get messages across. These are usually in addition to other methods. The management in some organizations hold events where a 'state of the nation' type of message is presented. If the organization is too big to make the presentation to everyone at the same time, a series of present- ations, or in the case of very dispersed organizations, 'road shows' have been held. In some organizations these events are held to coincide with the business planning process. At the event the previous year's performance is reviewed and the next year's plan launched.

We have found a number of organizations that have annual events off-site but these tend in the main to be smaller organizations. However, one larger organization, Raflatac, based in Scarborough, went as far as holding a conference to which all 230 employees, including those based in Stevenage and Dublin, were invited. As well as reviewing how the company had developed over the previous seven to eight years, a customer was invited to make a presentation of his views of the company's service and quality. It ended with a session where the senior management team sat on stage and answered questions from the floor.

Communication skills needed by managers

To carry out the roles mentioned above, managers need the follow- ing communication skills:

- presentational skills;
- questioning skills;
- listening skills;
- chairing meetings;
- clarifying to check understanding.

Communication, managers and the trade unions

We have found that, in organizations that are working towards Investors in People recognition and which recognize trade unions, the relationship between management and unions is frequently quite cooperative. Many have found that such relationships improve as they involve the trade unions in the process, usually through participation in working groups. Good communication processes exist to keep the unions informed of achievements against plans and future developments, often at an early stage.

Generally we have found relationships with trade unions are managed by senior staff unless organizations are very big and geographically dispersed, where local arrangements are made involving local managers.

Some organizations that do not recognize trade unions use Staff Representative Committees to consult or canvass for staff opinions and pass on information to employees. Members of these committees are often elected or nominated by their colleagues. They are expected to consult their colleagues before attending the meetings, so they do need to have some advance warning of the issues to be discussed in order to seek views. These types of committees may serve as Works Councils for those companies that need to meet EU legislative requirements.

What do managers need to do?

- Keep people informed about what the organization is trying to achieve and their contribution.
- Keep people informed about how well the organization is doing.
- Ensure people understand how their development contributes to the success of the team and the organization.
- Listen to concerns from employees and pass them back up to senior managers.
- Keep people informed about development opportunities and encourage them to take them up.
- Take steps to show people that their contribution and achievements have been recognized and that they are appreciated.

- Continually reinforce the above messages.
- Demonstrate commitment to people and their development.

Summary

This chapter has examined communication as a process. It has considered why communication with the workforce is needed and how it reinforces commitment from the top to train and develop the workforce. It has detailed the methods used by some organizations and the role of managers and the skills they need in order to deliver the required Investors in People outcomes.

CHAPTER 6

Identifying Learning, Training and Development Needs

This chapter relates to a vital stage in managing the development of people and is key to delivering the required outcomes and therefore plays an important part in determining whether an organization will meet the requirements of Investors in People. It examines the involvement of the manager in the identification of training and development needs of individuals and of their team. It starts off by examining the extended training and development cycle. Next it looks at a number of methods used to identify training and development needs. It then examines planning for evaluation through the setting of objectives, targets and standards for training and development actions.

The (extended) training and development cycle

The first issue in managing the process is to have a helpful framework or structure. Within the Investors in People Standard there are a number of frameworks made up by linking the evidence requirements (see Appendix 1 for the full list of indicators and

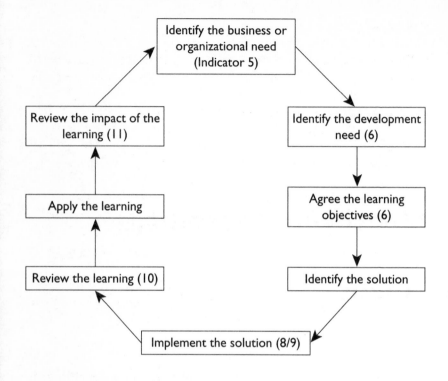

Figure 6.1 *The extended training and development cycle*

evidence requirements). For the purpose of managing the training and development process we have called this 'the extended training and development cycle' (see Figure 6.1).

Identifying individual training and development needs

In the previous chapter, as part of the communication model, we addressed the issue of identifying broad aims and communicating plans. This was also described in Chapter 4 when the role of senior managers was discussed. This of course sets the context for the next stage in the training cycle: identifying individual and team development needs.

Appraisal

The most commonly used method of identifying individual training needs is through an appraisal. An effective appraisal process should offer the opportunity to review what has happened since the previous appraisal, ie, whether agreed objectives were met but, more importantly, to look ahead to the next period by agreeing what is expected of the appraisee leading to the agreement on the next set of objectives, including training and development objectives.

We agree with the usual comments concerning appraisal:

- it should be motivational;
- it should formalize what good managers have been informally doing throughout the period, such as monitoring of work, coaching and giving feedback as required, so there should be no surprises;
- it should include recognition and praise where it is due;
- it should allow the appraisees the opportunity to have their say, including commenting on their feelings.

Appraisal is an opportunity to communicate and reinforce the vision and mission of the organization (and values where they exist) and clarify how the individual contributes to its success. These also set the context for the appraisal itself as in most organizations training and development should be focused on helping to meet the business or organizational objectives.

However, we do have concerns about appraisal as a vehicle for identifying training and development needs. In practice what often happens is that one or two questions are added to the end of the appraisal such as: 'Do you feel you have any training needs?', 'What training would you like?' This leads to the delivery of training and development relating to what people think they want rather than what they and their manager agree they need and inevitably leads to what is commonly referred to as a 'wish list' (ie, training activities that have little relevance to helping the organization achieve its objectives). We return to this issue later in this chapter.

In some organizations the appraisal process is often very complicated and time-consuming and is therefore seen by managers as a chore. If managers see it in this light they are likely to approach it with an inappropriate attitude and probably will not recognize that it is a process that should be beneficial to them as well as the appraisee. It is inevitable that the appraisal process will come into disrepute in these circumstances.

In many organizations appraisals are linked to performance and therefore to pay or merit bonus. In the Civil Service, in spite of many attempts to separate the issues, they were linked to an individual's 'promotability'. This tends to distract both the appraiser and the appraisee from the opportunity to have a meaningful discussion about training and development needs.

Finally, we have concerns about the effectiveness of training for appraisers, which often concentrates on the appraisal process rather than the skills needed to carry it out effectively.

Training and development reviews

In some organizations the 'A' word – appraisal – is not well received.

The Investors in People Standard does not require organizations to have an appraisal process; rather it requires as part of the planning process that:

- the organization has clear priorities which link the development of people to its aims and objectives at organization, team and individual level (indicator 6);
- top management can describe strategies that they have put in place to support the development of people in order to improve the organization's performance (indicator 1);
- people can give examples of how they have been encouraged to improve their own performance (indicator 2);
- people clearly understand what their development activities should achieve, both for them and for the organization (indicator 6);
- . . . receive appropriate and constructive feedback on a timely and regular basis (indicator 3).

An effective appraisal process clearly will deliver the above outcomes.

Many organizations choose, for differing reasons, to introduce a process of training and development reviews referred to in many organizations as 'Performance Development Reviews' (PDRs). They have many different names but essentially they carry out a similar function – to help managers identify the (training and) development needed to enable the individual to carry out their role.

The process is usually kept as simple as possible and consists of a short one-to-one interview which focuses on the skills and knowledge the person needs to carry out the job and whether there is a need for further development of those skills and knowledge. Some organizations may offer development opportunities beyond the needs of the individual's job in the belief that any type of development will have a spin-off on the motivation of the individual. This may sometimes get the person back into the habit of learning which can subsequently encourage the desire to develop in the workplace.

On some occasions it may not be practical to carry out one-to-one interviews. Some organizations have decided to carry out group training and development reviews. While this is not ideal it can work when the groups of people are carrying out very similar roles and provided the process offers an opportunity for people to discuss their *individual* needs, in private if necessary.

Job analysis, standards, competencies, etc

Appraising or assessing training and development needs raises the issue of against what does the manager assess? Many organizations use job analyses; others have standards and/or competencies.

While the concept of job analysis is not new, the issue of competence is. When organizations have used job analysis in the past it has usually been led by training departments. Today, managers are increasingly becoming more involved in the use of these processes. The concept involves breaking down jobs into simple stages or tasks. Each stage is written down with the various actions that have to be undertaken. When a person is trained to do the job, the analysis can be used by the trainer as a 'script' to ensure that the person is trained properly and given to the trainee as an aide mémoire.

As part of their approach to quality (often linked to the ISO 9000 series), a number of organizations have included job analyses in their quality manuals, sometimes in the form of checklists. As part of the quality procedures trainees have to be 'signed off' as being able to complete the job satisfactorily. An extract from a sample checklist is included in Figure 6.2.

The concept of competence takes this a stage further. Increasingly, organizations are considering the use of National Vocational Qualifications (NVQs) as a method of assessing the competence of existing employees or developing new skills and then assessing the competence. Although some people would criticize NVQs as being bureaucratic and sometimes too broad, the competencies and standards within the NVQs, which are described as performance criteria, can be used in a variety of ways and in particular to identify training and development needs.

A number of organizations that have used NVQs have trained their managers as assessors, which has had a spin-off in developing their people management skills too. Needless to say, there are NVQs for assessors. (For those who are interested in finding out more about NVQs, see Appendix 2, Qualifications and Curriculum Authority.)

NVQs have also been developed for managers; for up-to-date information contact the Management Charter Initiative office (see Appendix 2). They also produce material about the relevance of the management standards to organizations working towards Investors in People status.

Personal development plans

As an outcome of appraisal or training reviews some organizations, or sometimes managers within organizations, encourage employees to draw up a personal development plan, sometimes called an 'individual development plan'. Personal development plans come in a range of formats but basically they comprise written document-ation that highlights what actions have been agreed at the appraisal/review. They can be very elaborate or kept very simple. At their simplest they would include:

- the purpose of the training or development action(s);
- the objectives of the action(s);
- the methodology to be used to meet the action(s);
- the date by which the action(s) should be started;

		Assessed as satisfactory	

SAFE WORKING PROCEDURE

Area: Slab Grinding Bay

Activity: Abrasive Wheel Mounting

Hazards: Restricted space; Heat from wheel stub

Protective equipment required:
        Safety helmet and boots, gloves, safety jacket and trousers

Equipment required:
        Wheel change device; torque wrench; hand hammer
        Pneumatic spanner and socket; wooden wedges

Methodology:

Main wheel (two-man job)

Methodology	Assessed as satisfactory	
	Yes	No
1. Set machine in correct position, head back until wheel centrally over track.		
2. Isolate machine, release air pressure to wheel head, switch on power to wheel change device.		
3. Wedge wheel collet with wooden wedges to prevent it turning and slacken all 8 wheel bolts with torque wrench.		
4. Run bolts loose with pneumatic spanner, remove and take out wedges.		
5. Locate wheel change device on to central collect and lock. Withdraw and lower collet. Lift off old stub manually and discard. (Dropping stub may damage table ropes.)		
6. Clean round wheel periphery to remove swarf, etc. Check explosion guard in good condition and safe.		
7. Place new wheel on wheel stand. Fit new packings to front and rear of collet and locate collet on to new wheel. Turn over locking bars to secure wheel changing device.		
8. Lift wheel and manipulate into position. Slide wheel into collet and when fully home secure with one stud.		
9. Release locking bars, release collet securing lock and withdraw wheel changing device and return to its original position.		

(Adapted from SMACC, AvestaPolarit Sheffield, Unit Trainer)

Figure 6.2 *A sample checklist*

- the date by which the outcome from the action(s) should be reviewed, ie, were objectives met?

Ideally the plans should include long, medium and short-term objectives but this may vary depending on the complexity of the person's job.

An example of a personal development plan for a manager is included in Figure 6.3.

Purpose	Objectives	Methodology	Action from	Reviewed by
To be able to chair team meetings	To develop 'facilitation' skills – listening skills – controlling the meeting – summarizing skills	1. Attendance on chairing meetings course 2. Shadow manager at regional meetings 3. Observation and feedback by manager	January February Throughout March	February End of February April
To create more time to 'supervise' the team	To develop time management systems To identify tasks that can be delegated	Attend time management module Coaching from manager	March Throughout April	End of March Early May
To improve written reports so that report writing can be delegated by manager	To develop planning skills To be able to write in an appropriate style	Coaching and feedback from manager Review colleagues' reports for style and presentation	Middle of May Immediately	End of June Middle of may

Figure 6.3 *Example of a personal development plan*

Identifying team training and development needs

The most frequently used method of identifying the training and development needs of teams is the training (or skills) matrix. Investors in People assessors are often presented with a training matrix as a method used to identify individual needs but unless they are very sophisticated (and therefore complex) they usually don't address the needs of individuals.

The most common reason for their use is that managers can see at a glance whether they have sufficient people trained in the range of tasks for which their team is responsible. An example of a training matrix is shown in Figure 6.4.

People: Job	Tom	Frances	Elaine	Erroll	Jagvinder	Claire
Ledger	***	**		*		
Accounts	***	***	*			
Payroll	***	*	**			
Purchasing	***	***		**		
Timesheets	***			**		
Computer:						
Word	**	***	*	*		***
Excel	***	**			***	
Access	*		***			***
E-mail	***	***	**	*	**	*
Post duties		***	***	*		**

Key: *** Fully trained; ** Currently being trained; * Future training need

Figure 6.4 *Example of a training matrix*

The example shows that on one axis of the matrix are listed the tasks the team have to perform and on the other a list of the people. To keep the illustration simple, the example merely shows who has been trained, who is undergoing training and who has been identified as needing training. Managers could develop the process to include symbols that show the degree of competence of the individuals and it is at this stage that they begin to address the needs of individuals.

Training matrices are of course not a new idea but quite often we have found that they are documents used by managers and kept in the manager's office, and employees never see them. What Investors in People has done has challenged this communications issue. Why should they be kept hidden away? Why shouldn't the team have the opportunity to be involved in the development of the matrix? Where team members are involved in the process they become more motivated and more willing to learn new tasks because they can see why it is necessary. They may also understand better why some training they have asked for as an individual is unlikely to take place as they can see that there are sufficient people trained to do the task to meet the needs of the team. They may not like it but they can understand it!

The manager's role versus the role of training specialists

Chapter 2 noted that in most organizations managers have the responsibility to identify training and development needs and are supported by the training specialist(s), where they exist. The processes listed above need to be kept as simple as possible if managers are to use them.

Investors in People assessors will not expect managers to be experts in training and development, but they will expect them to have a broad awareness of and use some of the various management tools that are available to help them, so that they can fulfil their responsibilities. That is why we have consistently said that where training and/or development specialists exist, they are there to support managers, not to replace them or their functions. This support can be offered in many ways:

- to help managers develop an awareness of needs and perhaps develop the tools and techniques that are needed to identify them;
- to help carry out the identification of needs where a more detailed analysis is needed;
- to provide information or direct to sources of information where necessary, eg, training providers, course information, college prospectuses;
- to deliver training;
- to advise and perhaps set up evaluation systems to help managers assess the effectiveness of the training.

Planning for evaluation of training and development

As evaluation is often seen as the most difficult part of becoming an Investor in People, it is important to plan.

As indicated in the extended training cycle, planning for evaluation of training and development starts with the organization's need or objectives:

- What is the organization trying to achieve?
- What skills or knowledge do people need to help the organization achieve its objective?
- What skills or knowledge do people already have?
- Is there a gap between what is needed and what people already have?
- What do people therefore need to learn to be able to do?
- How will you know that they can do it?

An illustration may help clarify. The organizational need is to increase efficiency and therefore profitability. One method of doing this may be to increase the flexibility of the workforce. An examination of current working practice shows that most people are only able to do one job effectively. They do not support each other at times of pressure; in fact some people can be standing around while others are working flat out. You know that this needs to change.

You will know that you have achieved this change when all people are able to carry out at least two functions and people automatically help one another out when under pressure. The people therefore need to learn extra knowledge and skills and teams need to be built.

Going through this process makes it easier to develop objectives.

Setting and agreeing objectives, targets and standards for training and development activities

If you don't know what you want, how can you know when you've got it?

Investors in People assessors often find that organizations and their managers have difficulties with evaluation because they are poor at objective setting.

We have found that poorly constructed training and development objectives are usually vague. Vague objectives are usually not objectives at all, but aims, ie, broad statements of what is required.

One example of a vague objective we found concerned training for a receptionist where the objective that had been agreed was: 'to improve reception skills'. A course had been identified and the person was ready to go. When the manager of the receptionist was asked how she would know when the receptionist's skills had improved, the answer at first was as vague as the objective. However, with further probing it transpired that the receptionist did not have a weakness in the skills needed in dealing with customers (the subject of the course) either by phone or in person; rather she was unable to answer the questions posed by customers. She constantly had to consult other people for information, which did not look very professional to customers and caused interruptions for the people she consulted. The need was not for improved reception skills but for increased knowledge about the organization and its services. Therefore the manager would know that the training need had been addressed when the receptionist's knowledge had increased and she was more self-sufficient. The training course was cancelled and internal arrangements were made to increase her knowledge.

This may seem an extreme example but it is a true one. It raises the question, if objectives are not clarified, how often do people go on the wrong course? Setting the criteria for learning in advance is very important. Some of the issues to consider are shown in Figure 6.5.

Sometimes objectives may exist in the minds of the people concerned but are not written down, discussed and agreed. Investors in People does not require objectives to be written down and it may be perfectly acceptable to agree objectives verbally; however, there is less room for misunderstanding if they are written down. When it comes to evaluating whether the objectives have been achieved, it is also much easier to check if they are in writing.

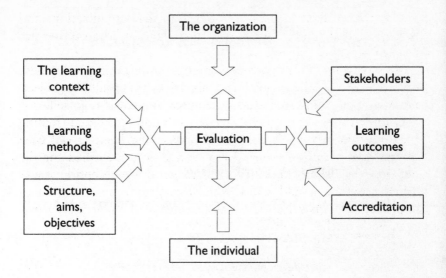

Figure 6.5 *Setting criteria*

Objectives can be made clearer and more specific by simply asking the question, 'How will I know when the person demonstrates the new skill or applies the newly acquired knowledge?'

Training specialists often refer to 'SMART' objectives. The initials stand for Specific, Measurable, Achievable, Realistic and Timebound. An example of a SMART objective for training the receptionist mentioned above would be:

> By the end of the training session, the receptionist would be able to demonstrate that she has the knowledge to answer 10 questions on the five main services offered by the organization.

It is also possible that readers will come across a similar acronym summarizing how to set objectives: SUMATRA. The key addition is that it emphasizes understanding: Specific, Understood, Measurable, Agreed, Timebound, Realistic and Achievable. To illustrate further, there are examples of aims and objectives for a workshop on the subject of this book given in Figure 6.6.

To be even more specific and therefore make objectives more measurable, targets and standards can be built into the objectives. Targets normally refer to quantity, eg, 'to be able to make 50 widgets

---

Investors in People Workshop
The Line Manager's Role in Investors in People

Aim:
To ensure line managers understand the role an assessor will expect them to play in helping the organization to achieve the Investors in People Standard.

Objectives:
By the end of the workshop participants will:

- Understand which indicators their actions affect and how they can help the organization meet the Standard.
- Have increased their understanding of the Investors in People Standard and its indicators.
- Understand what 'development' is in an Investors in People context.
- Have identified any barriers that may stop them carrying out the role required.
- If there are barriers they will have identified methods of overcoming them.

Figure 6.6 *Example of aims and objectives for a workshop*

an hour' or, 'to type at 50 words per minute'. Standards normally refer to quality, eg, 'to be able to produce financial forecasts to 100 per cent accuracy' or, 'to be able to produce widgets to tolerances of 0.01 cm'.

Customers often define standards and, as mentioned earlier in this chapter, organizations with quality procedures usually write the quality standards into the quality manual. The checklists also mentioned earlier (see Figure 6.2) will probably include standards that determine whether or not a person is competent. When it comes to written work, most organizations have a house style or corporate image – another type of standard.

Value statements, customer charters, perhaps even mission statements, may define organizational standards. However, when it comes to personal standards it is more difficult. Managers will have their own standards and unfortunately these may vary from one manager to another. It is therefore important that managers clearly communicate what their standards are. Some managers are frequently dissatisfied with work produced by members of staff – this is often because they have not defined what they expect, ie, the standard. Personal standards are often difficult to describe. For example, in written work it may be as simple as having certain phrases or words that they would like their staff not to use.

Communication, coaching and feedback are the keys to ensuring that employees know what the standards are and are trained to deliver to those standards. Good practice would suggest that part of the manager's role prior to any development activity is therefore to have a discussion to ensure that the person knows why they are undertaking the training or development activity, and to clarify that what the manager expects the person to be able to do following the event is the same as the trainee's expectations. This briefing may be quite short in some cases, but ideally a note could be kept so that it can be referred to for evaluation after the event. Some organizations have produced a form (see Appendix 3), the first page of which can be used for this pre-event discussion. Again this type of paperwork is not essential to help demonstrate the required outcomes for Investors in People but it is helpful and avoids the need for people to rely on their memory.

What do managers need to do?

- Be aware of the needs of the organization.
- Carry out regular reviews of the (training and) development needs of their people in order that they are able to meet their performance objectives.
- Agree SMART objectives for training and developmental or learning activity before the activity takes place.

Summary

This chapter has examined the actions a manager would be expected to carry out in order to identify the training and development needs of individuals and their teams. It has included a model – the extended training cycle – and some examples of the methods used by some organizations. Finally, it has examined setting objectives for training and development activities.

CHAPTER 7

Identifying Solutions

Throughout this book we have very rarely mentioned training without also mentioning development. The Investors in People Standard refers to development but does not of course exclude training. Identifying training solutions is fairly straightforward in most organizations so this chapter concentrates on development. It starts by looking at definitions and continues by looking at some of the vast range of methods available to managers to develop their people.

Definition

The *Oxford English Dictionary* defines 'develop' as: 'to make or become larger or fuller or more mature or organized'. In the context of developing *people* there are many definitions. The definition we include uses words with a similar meaning to those in the dictionary definition: 'To broaden and enhance the skills, knowledge and attitudes of groups and individuals in order to maximize potential.'

The key words in this definition are *broaden, enhance* and *maximize potential*. These suggest that the act of developing people is to build on something that is already there. It is difficult, and perhaps unnecessary, to define the difference between training and development because they overlap so much. However, it is important to acknowledge that *all training is development but not all development is training.* Many managers tend to focus on training courses when faced with the need to help people develop skills. To some it may be the easy option but it may not be the most appropriate or the one with the greatest potential for success. To help managers consider what other options they have, this chapter concentrates on those aspects of development that are not training.

Another way to look at development is to look at it as 'learning'. In Taylor and Thackwray (2001a) we considered learning organizations and their relationship to Investors in People. Development is an integral part of the activity of a learning organization.

Development should involve stretching people to test out their potential. For people with lots of potential and/or ambition, this may involve a huge 'stretch'; for others it may simply be a short step. It may involve asking them to do something new; it may be merely building on something they already do.

Planning for development

Whatever the reason, development should be planned and structured. Inevitably, unplanned development opportunities will occur and it would be foolish not to take them up.

As with training, planned development should have a purpose, eg, to take on new or different responsibilities in order to test potential or encourage creativeness. It should have SMART/ SUMATRA objectives, as described in Chapter 6, and it should be structured. One way of giving it structure is to make it a 'development programme' or 'project'. This will be a series of linked activities, each supporting or building on one another. For example, an induction programme is a development 'programme' with the purpose of introducing new staff to the organization (and the organization to the new staff), its people and the individual's work. Induction often includes a training event as part of the 'programme'; so too could other types of development programme.

As described in Chapter 6, those being developed should be briefed prior to commencing the programme and the purpose and objectives agreed. Because some development projects may be spread over a period of time, plans to monitor progress should be agreed, with review dates entered in diaries.

To some managers this may appear to involve extra work. For some it may, but for many a lot of processes will already exist and may merely need refining. In Chapter 6 we referred to a variety of methods of identifying needs – appraisal, training and development reviews, and personal development plans. These are all vehicles to enable the manager to 'manage' development. However, in many organizations we have found that these processes concentrate on the traditional methods, ie, training courses, rather than considering alternative methods.

So what are the alternative methods?

Development activities

When reading the following section, many will find themselves saying, 'We do many of these things, so what's new?' Perhaps nothing, but could it be more structured? Can you evaluate its impact? (Chapter 9 will look at evaluating development.)

Increasingly organizations are developing intranets and their World Wide Web capacity, so many of the following methods could, either additionally or solely, be Web-based.

Reading

Most people will read and will 'learn'. For many people the only way of keeping up to date with the latest trends and ideas within their professions is to read newspapers, books, journals, etc. For others, reading reports is part of their job and for some, such as researchers perhaps, reading may be a large part of their job. Some people don't find the time to read while others may find the thought of having to read to learn off-putting as it is not their preferred style of learning. However, there is no doubt that reading is developmental and should be considered as one of the options when putting together a developmental programme.

Open learning

For those who do not like reading, perhaps open learning (sometimes referred to as 'distance' or 'flexible' learning) offers a more attractive alternative. There is a huge variety of open learning methodologies (reading itself is one) so we are concentrating on some of the most popular ones.

First there are audio and video tapes. Audio tapes are quite a useful and perhaps less time-consuming method as they could be played while driving; however, this does present difficulties if you want to make a note of key points.

There are a variety of computer-based training methods including tutorials that come with software packages, CD ROM interactive packages, etc. There are also still in use programme textbooks in some organizations but these have generally been replaced by computer-based or Web-based packages.

Discovery learning

Some people learn how to use computer software packages by this method – trial and error, trying out different commands to see what happens. For people who have a basic knowledge, perhaps those who have been on a training course, it is quite an appropriate method as computer packages are so complex, a training event cannot possibly cover all aspects. The same principles can be used in other ways. Some organizations use discovery learning as a method of induction – researching and interviewing people to learn about the organization. An advantage of discovery learning is that people are not being 'taught' but are 'learning' and are therefore more likely to retain the information or skills.

Observing, questioning, thinking, reviewing mistakes, etc

These to a large extent go hand in glove with discovery learning. Watching other people is probably the most common method of self-development; we do it all the time, but do we always think about it sufficiently and review what we've seen? This of course is especially important in the workplace because a lot of learning can take place by observing role models. However, to *understand* why people have done things in certain ways, or perhaps *not* done it in a certain way, it is necessary to ask questions.

It is often said that people are their own harshest critics. This is often because we know we could have done better. Sometimes we may feel this way even though everyone else said we did ok! Reflecting on what went well and what didn't go so well is a very powerful developmental tool, provided notes are kept, either mentally or in writing.

Shadowing, attachments, secondments, etc

These methods follow on from above. They can be long-term approaches, eg, six-month secondments, or short. They can have many different purposes, from widening knowledge and experience to learning how customers think.

Visits

A visit could be classed as an extremely short attachment. Visits as developmental opportunities appeared to fall into disuse for a while, but we have found that their use is increasing. They are often incorporated into continuous improvement strategies when visits are used for people from various parts of the organization to get to know customers, or help people understand what happens to their product once it leaves them. In the service sector they may be used as a method of finding out the best practice by observing what competitors are doing. If organizations are large and/or geographically dispersed, visits will serve to build teams and relationships. It is often helpful for administrators or shop floor workers to go out with sales reps on sales visits, or for administrators to visit the shop floor.

Attendance at conferences, exhibitions, etc

These of course are another sort of 'visit'. Many organizations encourage their people to attend this type of event to look at the latest ideas and technology, among other things. Quite often the purpose may be obvious, but are the outcomes always evaluated? Could they be more structured? If more than one person attends, is there duplication of effort? Some organizations only send senior people to such events. Would there be a benefit in sending more junior people or shop floor workers?

In some organizations there is a reluctance by some managers to encourage visits whether they be to other organizations or exhibitions. This is frequently because the managers simply don't trust their people to make full use of the visit for its intended purpose. Of course such activities could be open to abuse, but if the culture of the organization is one that encourages development or learning, the vast majority of people do not abuse these opportunities. Other managers say it's a perk. Of course visits are perks but people can learn from them and many managers find that when people return they apply what they've learnt. They are also often more motivated and frequently work harder to make up for the production time they lost.

Job swaps

Rather than just visit other parts of the organization, why not swap jobs for a short time? A good illustration of how useful this can be occurred in a company mentioned earlier: Raflatac. As part of a number of development initiatives, managers encouraged job swaps and as a result a member of the dispatch team ended up working in the sales office. He received a phone call from a customer complaining about the non-receipt of an urgent item. Apparently the previous night, as it was getting late, he had put aside the parcel 'as another day would not make a difference'. After dealing with the complaint he realized it did make a difference. This illustrates how job swaps help people understand the implications of their actions, or non-actions, and can lead to improvements in the quality of service.

Delegation

The correct use of delegation as a management tool should lead to lots of developmental opportunities. It can combine some of the benefits of job swaps, such as understanding the manager's role, with the opportunity to make people's jobs more interesting. Effective delegation involves a number of simple steps:

- Correct identification of the task to be delegated, eg, not high risk.
- Correct identification of the person to whom work is being delegated – are they capable? Are they willing?
- Briefing and coaching to ensure they know what they are expected to do, how to do it and what to do if they need help.
- Monitoring how they are doing but not too closely. If you can't trust them to get on with it you've probably chosen the wrong person.
- Being available if required.
- Reviewing what has been learnt.

Job rotation, rotating duties

Whereas delegation most likely involves the manager passing work down to staff, job rotation involves people doing other jobs at the same level. This can be particularly useful in areas where jobs are perhaps straightforward and rather boring, and people need motivating. Rotating duties is similar, but may be simply encouraging people to rotate who takes the minutes of meetings. It could include aspects of delegation and the manager could rotate who chairs the meeting. The guidelines for delegation should be followed.

Attending meetings, sharing information/ideas/good practice, etc

As most people attend meetings at some time or other, they are another developmental opportunity that readers may consider obvious. Not every meeting will be a learning opportunity: it is how the learning is assessed and used that is important.

Quality circles/improvement groups

While some organizations may consider quality circles a bit old fashioned, many use a variant of them, often referred to as 'continuous improvement groups'. They are used in a variety of ways, sometimes to solve problems, sometimes to generate new ideas and improve systems, etc as part of quality initiatives. They can involve a variety of methodologies such as brainstorming. Sometimes the 'learning' is difficult to assess as it is integrated with the improvements to processes, products and other improvements.

Some organizations empower their people to run and manage these types of groups and only involve managers when it is essential. These groups can therefore offer alternative development opportunities: to develop the skills associated with setting up groups, agreeing and circulating agendas, managing and/or chairing the groups, etc.

Special projects

In many organizations some improvement groups may be viewed as special projects, while in others the outcome may be to set up a project or pilot. Some projects may involve groups of people; others may just involve one person. They may form part of the action associated with another learning or development opportunity. They may be associated with a qualification such as an MBA.

Once again, evaluating the 'learning' from a project may not always be easy, but if it is planned properly it will have an evaluation strategy and it may be simple to set 'learning objectives' as part of the overall project plan.

'Is there another way?'

This question is usually associated with the Japanese approach known as 'Kaizen' – the search for a better way. Quality circles or improvement groups are one approach; there are others. They don't need to be complex. The traditional staff suggestion scheme is one method.

Some organizations encourage people to innovate, experiment or simply do something in a different way. Being creative and imaginative, turning things on their head, can all lead to lots of new ideas and approaches and involve lots of 'learning'. One example is HPC in Stevenage, Herts. It operates a scheme that promotes training and development activities beyond those that relate to business objectives as part of its commitment to lifelong learning. Following a recommendation from a colleague for helping/assisting with something 'above and beyond the call of duty', or for contributing to the in-house journal, points are awarded to a certain value. The tokens are exchangeable only for training and development activities.

Self-development

People, of course, should not need to wait for their managers to identify the need for development. All the above are options for people to choose for their own development, whether work related or not. Organizations that have, or are developing, a learning culture will create a climate whereby people *want* to learn and develop. Some organizations have been working towards developing this culture for some time. The Rover Group, for example, even set up a separate business, The Rover Learning Business, to help manage and provide opportunities for the development of employees.

Self-development sits comfortably with lifelong learning, which for a number of years has been promoted to encourage people to develop skills and knowledge in order to help them compete in what is often seen as a less secure working environment.

Personal development

Although everything mentioned above could be classed as personal development, it is largely development that is related to the needs of the person's organization. Personal development is clearly much wider than this. In these days of tight budgets, many organizations only support development that will lead to business benefits. There are, however, a number of organizations that do support more or less any kind of development activity as they believe it will encourage a learning climate. The Ford Motor Company has long had such a programme but it is not just large organizations that promote such schemes. Raflatac, which has been mentioned a number of times in this book, offers each of its employees £50 per year to spend as they wish on development. The original idea was that it should be used for college fees, but in practice it has been used in many different ways, eg, on driving lessons.

What do managers need to do?

- Be clear on the organization's strategy in terms of supporting development.
- Encourage employees by creating a 'learning climate'.
- Keep people informed about developmental opportunities, or be able to direct their employees to the source of such information.
- Support and encourage those employees who take up developmental opportunities.

Summary

This chapter has looked at where development fits in. It has attempted to define what development is and how it relates to the concept of a 'learning organization'. It has examined a selection of developmental activities and ended by looking at self-development and personal development.

CHAPTER 8

Implementing the Solutions

This chapter has great significance for the manager because it is about what should actually be *done*. We therefore go into some detail about the issues that managers need to be aware of in order to be effective. The emphasis is often on processes. If these processes are used effectively they should automatically deliver the outcomes required to become an Investor in People.

One of the Investors in People indicators states that: 'managers are effective in supporting the development of people' (indicator 6). It does not mean that managers have to do *everything* but it does mean they have to do *something*.

Effective support starts before the development activity and continues during and after it. Here we build on the previous chapters, which concerned effective support prior to the development activity. This chapter focuses on implementing the identified and development solutions.

It examines what managers should do to effectively support employees through the activity. It starts with induction for new employees and goes on to look at coaching and feedback. It links to Chapter 9, which examines the support following the development activity through evaluation.

Induction

Why bother?

Research has shown that the first few days and weeks are critical to the opinions formed by new employees of their new employer. Organizations that lose new employees quickly, even those 'grateful' for a job, inevitably lose them because the organization has not met their expectations. The costs of recruiting and selecting new employees are high, possibly as high as 25 per cent of salary, not only in terms of time and money but in disruption too. Anything that can be done to minimize this must be very welcome; induction should be a significant factor here.

Eight benefits of an effective induction

New starters will:

1. Be able to explain the organization's aims and objectives and see where their jobs fit in.
2. Know that the organization is committed to developing its employees and of future opportunities that may exist.
3. Be more likely to remain with the organization thus reducing employment costs by reducing labour turnover.
4. Be more motivated and able to be more effective – sooner.
5. Be aware of the need to promote quality or other key organizational values.
6. Build links with existing employees (eg, through mentoring/coaching schemes).
7. Be aware of the legal requirements and organizational policies on health and safety, equal opportunities, etc.
8. Be aware of organizational messages before getting locked into departmental or sectional loyalties.

What is induction?

The Arbitration, Conciliation and Advisory Service (ACAS) guidelines define induction as 'helping a new employee to settle down into a new job as soon as possible, by becoming familiar with the people, surroundings, job, and the firm and industry'.

Most people can recall how they have experienced poor induction and many may feel that it is a thing of the past; we have found that this is not the case. New starters are sometimes dropped in at the deep end with little information while others are overloaded with information about the organization and are introduced to *everybody* and *everything*. When it does take place, induction is often unstructured and poorly planned and may take little account of past experience.

Induction, or the introduction to the new organization, starts at recruitment. As the personnel role is devolved to managers they are becoming involved at the selection and interviewing stages. Some organizations, such as Hewlett Packard, encourage managers to contact new appointees before they start work so that the process of 'joining' the new organization starts early.

Induction courses, packs, etc

In many organizations induction is often seen as the 'induction course' or 'pack' that is presented to the new person on the first day. The problem with having induction courses is that they rely on having sufficient new starters to ensure courses are run frequently and are viable. In many organizations this is not the case and there are examples of people going on the induction course six months or even longer after they have started. The value of the course is lost and the person is probably not very motivated by such late induction no matter how valuable some parts of the course may be. Courses also suggest that induction is a one-off event when it should be seen as a continuing process. Graduate entry programmes are induction programmes and may last for a year or more.

To overcome the problem of courses that are infrequent or not viable, a number of organizations have developed induction packs, a type of open learning version of the induction course. However, what often happens with these packs is that they become an easy option: they are given to the new starter to work through with little guidance or support.

The manager's role in induction

The key responsibility is to identify requirements (ie, the nature, scope, depth) and then to see that they are met. People who have never had a job before or those who have been out of the job market for some time are likely to have differing needs to those who are changing employers. These needs should be clarified and for some people a type of appraisal or training review may be appropriate. New employees, even at more senior levels, will need induction although they may have to take more responsibility for organizing it themselves.

How much of the induction the manager actually delivers personally will vary from manager to manager. First-line managers will clearly be more involved than middle and senior managers. However, even very senior managers should have a role to play as induction offers an opportunity for them to demonstrate their commitment to training and development.

Effective support for induction means that the manager has a role to play whether there is a course or a pack, even if initially it is only to welcome the person to the organization. If managers delegate responsibility for delivering induction they should ensure that the inductor has the knowledge and skills to carry it out effectively. A checklist of the more common topics that should be considered by managers when designing induction programmes is given below.

Planning and delivering induction – the issues to consider for inclusion

Although local priorities and needs will vary to some extent, it is clear that there are six key areas that induction should address. They are:

1. the job;
2. personnel issues;
3. the department/unit/section;
4. other departments/units/sections;
5. the organization;
6. the area.

These are examined in more detail below. Clear lines of accountability should link each of these areas and their component elements to a particular function (ie, manager, colleague, mentor, personnel, other). The methodology should also be agreed (ie, mode of delivery – documents, face-to-face, visits, formal induction, other).

Line managers should ensure that all are addressed in full, either via the corporate induction programme, or local induction. The appraisal process must incorporate an opportunity for the new member of staff and his or her line manager to reflect on the contribution made to individual and departmental development by induction.

1. The job
The line manager must ensure that the new member of staff is supported in gaining knowledge of:

* duties, responsibilities, workload;
* standards and expectations;
* accommodation;
* resources;
* sources of information and support including arrangements for allocation of mentors/coaching arrangements;
* useful contacts.

2. Personnel issues
The line manager must ensure that the new member of staff is supported in gaining knowledge of:

* pay and pensions;
* hours and holidays;
* sickness and leave;
* appraisal;
* promotion;
* discipline, complaints and grievance procedures;
* trade unions and professional associations;
* staff support and counselling;
* staff benefits;
* financial matters.

3. The department, unit, section
The line manager must ensure that the new member of staff is supported in gaining knowledge of:

* structure and management;
* plans and activities;

- resources;
- people;
- policies and procedures;
- communications;
- facilities;
- geography;
- equipment;
- health and safety;
- personal and professional development opportunities (local and corporate).

4. Other departments/units/sections

The line manager must ensure that the new member of staff is supported in gaining knowledge of:

- purpose and activities;
- structure;
- communications;
- contacts;
- policies and procedures;
- geography;
- facilities and resources.

5. The organization

The line manager must ensure that the new member of staff is supported in gaining knowledge of:

- history and mission;
- structure and management;
- planning;
- funding;
- activities and resources;
- people;
- communications;
- facilities, especially parking, crèche, medical, catering, social policies and procedures, especially equal opportunities, health and safety, quality assurance, financial regulations, geography, calendar.

6. The area

The line manager must ensure that the new member of staff is supported in gaining knowledge of:

- geography;
- transport;
- accommodation;
- facilities;
- personal needs.

Alternative induction strategies

CD ROM/interactive video/intranet

Although these may be considered a type of pack, we thought it worth highlighting them as a number of larger organizations have developed their own multimedia packages that new employees can work through. Some are designed to be spread over a period of time and encourage the involvement of line managers through the setting of tests that they should review with the inductee.

Mentoring/coaching/buddy systems, etc

The mentor (or 'starter's friend' or 'buddy') is a response that should allow each new person access to the information they need, when they need it, in a form they can handle. The degree of formality adopted by different organizations varies widely, from very casual attachment, to a nominated trainer with responsibilities under the probationary procedures. Critical issues here include the preparation, selection and support of those staff who will act as mentors, as well as support for the (unfortunately titled) 'mentees'. This is especially crucial during the all-important first six weeks. Having a mentor or buddy who is not a manager allows the opportunity for the new starter to ask naive questions without embarrassment. In some organizations we have found that mentors can have more empathy with new starters if they are recent inductees, suitably trained of course.

'Discovery' learning

To avoid overloading new employees with too much information and to help people *learn* rather than be *told*, some organizations or their managers have developed a different approach to induction. This involves the inductee having to discover information about the organization through research or interviewing people. The new person would be briefed and pointed in the right direction then debriefed afterwards. This method offers various opportunities, especially when associated with other more traditional induction methods.

Changing job/role within the same organization

At a number of recent events we have been involved in, a straw poll of participants showed a significant number of them felt that they had experience of being 'dropped in it' when they had changed jobs within organizations. It seems that some managers, at all levels within organizations, assume that people who take up a new role, whether it is through promotion or level transfer, do not need any kind of introduction or support to carry out the new job. The most dangerous thing any manager can do is assume anything. Some people say that the word assume means 'It makes an ass out of u and me'.

When someone changes jobs the first thing that should be carried out is a training and development review, from which a development plan can be drawn up. What happens in practice is that the appraisal or review process is often put on hold until the person has settled into the new job. We have found that some people who have changed jobs have not had an appraisal or review for 18 months or more! The line manager has a clear responsibility to ensure that this does not happen.

Existing employees

The previous chapter described the actions a manager should take prior to development taking place. Depending what the development actions involve, the line manager will have certain responsibilities to carry out while they are taking place.

The first responsibility is to ensure that, when a need has been identified and objectives agreed, the action actually takes place. All too often we have found that for various reasons, but usually due to work pressures, needs are not met. If work constantly gets in the way of meeting training and development needs then the

Investors in People assessor will question the commitment of either the organization, the line manager, or both. If the training and development is needed then it should take place. Clearly not all needs can be met immediately but over a period of time they should be.

Managing the 'wish list'

In the previous chapter we raised the issue of appraisal identifying a 'wish list' of training and/or development that the individual wants rather than needs. This is a difficult job for managers but the Investors in People Standard offers a coherent framework which should help managers with this task.

Most organizations do not have unlimited resources for training and development. The focus therefore should always be on training and development that contributes to the organization's business objectives. Whenever an employee identifies a need the manager should encourage them to say why they think it helps meet these objectives. If the process of relating training and development to business needs is constantly adopted, some of the more extreme 'needs' will not be raised. The following describes an example of a dialogue between an employer and employee to illustrate this issue.

During the course of a training review, a Domestic Assistant in a nursing home asked if she could be trained as a flower arranger. The Matron, who was carrying out the review, asked how it would help the organization. The Domestic Assistant pointed out that it was important that the home was made pleasant and homely for residents and that prospective customers, when visiting the home, saw that this was the case. Arranging flowers contributed to this objective. The home from time to time brought in and paid a qualified flower arranger so there were potential savings if the Domestic Assistant could do it. The Matron decided that the training should take place.

Investors in People requires organizations to identify at organizational level what training and development is required to meet business needs. This too can offer a steer to employees if it is communicated to them. When individuals create 'wish lists', we have found that it is because employees are unaware of the organization's priorities for training and development.

Finally, if all else fails, do what the Food and Beverage Manager at the Renaissance Hotel, Heathrow did – present the wish list to the staff for them to decide what the priorities were.

Actively supporting

When it has been decided that the training or developmental need will be met, if the need is being met off-the-job it is unlikely that the line manager will have anything to do until the person returns. Post-development activity will be dealt with in Chapter 9.

If the need is being met on-the-job, the line manager support may entail either keeping a watching brief if the training has been delegated to an on-the-job trainer; or direct coaching and/or feedback by the line manager.

Keeping a watching brief

As line managers are responsible for training and development, even if they have delegated the delivery to another person within their team, they need to ensure that the delivery is effective. This can be done in a variety of ways but the most important is that they should ensure that the person delivering it is capable. This may mean coaching and feedback to the trainer themselves and perhaps some monitoring in the initial stages, especially if the trainer is relatively inexperienced. Some organizations, such as Airedale Springs Ltd (which features as a case study in Taylor and Thackwray, 2001b), have encouraged managers (or anyone involved in delivering training) to undertake train-the-trainer training in order to ensure that training and development is delivered effectively.

With any task that is being managed, the line manager should be available to handle any difficulties that arise. Once the delivery activity is completed the manager should carry out the post-development activity.

Coaching

This is one of the most important roles a line manager has in the development of people.

The *Oxford English Dictionary* defines a coach as 'a person who trains or teaches'. We would define coaching as: 'the process by which an individual trains or teaches another person, usually on a one-to-one basis and on-the-job, through the sharing of skills and knowledge in order to guide them to better results'.

The coach does not always have to be a line manager but all line managers should be able to coach. Coaching is usually a process rather than an event. Although it can be spontaneous it should be planned; good coaches would constantly be watching out for opportunities to coach, but they would also ensure that it is structured.

To be a successful coach, managers should be:

- good facilitators, ie, ask questions to check knowledge and understanding rather than tell people how and what to do;
- good listeners;
- able to use silence;
- observant;
- knowledgeable about the subject;
- encouraging, good motivators;
- credible;
- willing to take risks.

The coaching process involves the following:

- spotting opportunities and preparing;
- checking existing knowledge and understanding;
- remembering to tell – show – do, ie:
  - tell – the person what you're going to do and why and what they should be able to do after the activity
  - show – the person how to do it
  - do – get the person to do it;
- checking understanding;
- asking the person to do it again;
- monitoring progress once satisfied that they can do it, but not too closely, to avoid showing distrust.

Feedback

The ability to give feedback goes hand-in-hand with coaching skills.

The *Oxford English Dictionary* defines feedback as, 'The return of information to its supplier', so in a training and development context the definition could be: 'A communication process to an individual (or group) to inform them how their actions/behaviour affects others.'

The purpose of feedback is to *help* people learn/change behaviour.

When to give feedback

Feedback will often be given in formal situations, such as appraisal interviews, a training course following role plays, etc, or during coaching sessions. However, there may be times in informal situations such as a review of a meeting or presentation, when it may be appropriate to offer feedback. Both formal and informal situations involve a type of appraisal, or assessment; however, the major difference concerns the expectations of the recipient of the feedback.

In formal situations the recipient will expect to be given feedback because that is often a major part of the purpose of the situation. In informal situations, because the recipient may not expect feedback, it may be best to offer feedback, rather than give it. If the person refuses the feedback, but you feel it is important, then you may have to agree an appropriate time to give it.

Feedback and the use of competencies, standards, etc

In all these situations the feedback should follow observation and analysis of performance. This implies that the giver of the feedback should have some criteria, competence or standards against which to judge the person's performance. It is important to the receiver of the feedback that they understand in advance what these criteria are, especially in the formal situation. This links back to the job analysis, competencies, etc, discussed in Chapter 6.

In the informal situation, there may be times when the recipient does not know the criteria and this needs to be taken into account when offering the feedback.

Good practice

- Set the right 'climate'.
- Choose the right time, ie, not last thing at night or following a stressful event.
- Establish mutual trust between the giver and recipient. This is not always easy when you are the 'boss' and the receiver is a member of your staff.
- Handle resistance to change; as in any change situation it is likely that there could be some resistance or discomfort.
- Adopt a 'helping mode' of joint exploration.
- Ask the person *how they think they did* before telling them how you think they did. This often avoids confrontations if the person thinks they did well and you don't. If they do think they did well ask them, 'What was it that went well? What could you do differently?' This ensures that they know *why* it went well and that it was not just good luck.
- Concentrate on listening to their comments before giving feedback; most people are more critical of themselves than you would be and they will probably give you a lead on which to build your feedback.

Some useful tips

Formula for successful feedback

- Observe the behaviour.
- Analyse the behaviour – look for strengths as well as weaknesses.
- Feed back: reinforce what was good as well as areas for improvement, check the reaction and agree the desired behaviour.
- Support in order to change to the desired behaviour.

Remember *OAFS*.

Constructive feedback

- *Descriptive rather than evaluative* – it should describe what was observed in an objective manner. Evaluative feedback is likely to be subjective.

- *Specific rather than general* – focus on specific issues and illustrate with examples.
- *Avoid prescription* – what works for you may not always work for another person. Try to get the person to suggest what they will do differently so that they will 'own' the change in behaviour. However, if there is only one way to do something then prescription may be unavoidable.
- *Focus on modifiable behaviour* – it's no use focusing on issues that cannot be changed such as personality, stammers, etc.
- *Well timed* – it should be given *almost* immediately. Allow time for the person to reflect on their performance. However, if it is left too long the person may not recall enough about their performance to make the feedback worthwhile.
- *Balanced* – identify both strengths and weaknesses. Try not to be over-critical or to praise too much. Avoiding 'overload' is important: people can only tackle so many issues at once. When there are many issues it is important to focus on the appropriate or urgent ones. The other, less urgent, issues can be tackled later.
- *Validated with the receiver* – check understanding with the recipient of the feedback. Unless you do this the recipient may not change behaviour in the expected way.

Traps to avoid

- Starting your feedback with the words, 'If I were you. . .'. This usually means: 'If I were you (which I'm not) I would do it like this (which you did not)'.
- Giving unsolicited feedback – a lot of people like to give feedback but this is the type that is often ignored or could lead to disagreements and you enter a 'defend/attack' situation.
- Denying a person's feelings – if people say they feel a certain way then that is the way they feel.
- Raising irrelevant issues – eg, a person who is being coached on telephone-handling skills scratches their head or blinks a lot. It may be accurate feedback, but is it relevant?
- Goal-centred feedback – usually describes what should have happened rather than what did happen. This type of feedback does not take account of where the person is now!

- Allowing the person to become dependent on you – the idea of giving feedback is to enable the person to adopt the agreed behaviour. They may need some further support but not to the extent that they are reliant on you.

What do managers need to do?

- Ensure all new employees are inducted to their job.
- Identify the skills and knowledge that employees need in order to do their jobs.
- Review the skills and knowledge that employees have.
- Encourage employees to identify their own development solutions.
- Provide (or guide to) information about development opportunities, including access to qualifications as appropriate.
- Agree appropriate action to fill any gaps that employees may have in terms of skills or knowledge.
- Ensure the agreed action takes place.
- Agree desired outcomes ('learning objectives') before the action commences.
- Support the action as appropriate, eg, through coaching and feedback, including recognition and praise when appropriate.
- Check that the action has been successful and that the new skills and knowledge can be applied.
- Check that the new skills or knowledge are being applied and are having the desired results.
- If not, start the above cycle again.

Summary

This chapter has examined what effective support by the manager actually involves. It has looked at support for induction processes for new employees and job changers. It has looked at supporting the needs of existing employees and how to manage the 'wish list'. Finally, it has looked at coaching and feedback skills, an important part of active support.

CHAPTER 9

Reviewing and Applying the Learning

This chapter looks at delivering the outcomes required of what is perceived as the most challenging part of Investors in People – evaluation. We contend that it is impossible for effective evaluation to take place without careful planning and the setting of clear objectives in advance of any training and/or development. We look at the different approaches and mechanisms used by a range of organizations to evaluate training and development, with special reference to Investors in People. Included are details of the manager's role in evaluation and the gathering of information to enable the organization to ascertain the effectiveness of the development. Readers wanting further, in depth, information and guidance on evaluation tools, techniques and strategies should look at our companion book (Taylor and Thackwray, 2001b), Chapters 12–16 inclusive.

What is evaluation?

The *Oxford English Dictionary* defines to evaluate as: 'to find out or state the value of, to assess'. This definition is most appropriate when looking at evaluating training and development, especially in relation to Investors in People.

To evaluate the effectiveness of the training and development the questions following from the 'learning achieved' outlined in Figure 9.1 need to be addressed. These questions relate, in sequence, to the Investors in People indicators 10 and 11 in particular but also link to indicator 12.

the 'business' need ⬇	What is the organization/team/individual trying to achieve? How will you know when it is achieved?
the learning need ⬇	What do people need to learn to do differently? Will this involve developing knowledge, skills or a change of behaviour and/or attitude?
the 'development' action ⬇	What was the development activity?
the learning achieved ⬇	Has knowledge or skill increased as planned as a result of the action? How?
the impact on performance ⬇	So what difference has it made? Are people using the new skills or knowledge as planned? What is the impact on the individual/team and/or organization? Have behaviours/attitudes changed? How? So what?
The benefits?	Is the performance of the individual/team or organization better as a result of staff development? In what way?
Reduced costs?	What are they? How much? Time savings? What are they?
Value for money?	Increased effectiveness? How was it achieved? Increased efficiency?

Figure 9.1 *The evaluation 'audit' trail and questions to consider*

The 'So what?' questions towards the end of the model are extremely important. For example:

- The training and development activity met its objectives of helping trainees to learn a range of new skills. . . *So what?*
- The people are now able to do more than one job. . . *So what?*
- People are more flexible and instead of sitting around waiting for work to come in, can help colleagues to do other jobs. . . *So what?*
- The organization (or team) benefits because work is completed more quickly, temporary staff are not needed to cover for absence, holidays, etc, and therefore there is a clear cash saving.

Obviously the above process starts with a comparison between what was planned and what was achieved. Without objectives to compare achievements against, evaluation becomes at best subjective and often a rationalization.

A close examination of the above questions will reveal they are a mirror image of those posed in Chapter 6 where we looked at *planning* for evaluation. Another, complementary, way for managers to look at evaluation is to ask the following questions:

- Did the person enjoy the event?
- Did they learn anything?
- Did they transfer the learning to the workplace?
- Did the business benefit?

Frequently the only questions asked are the first two. There is also a danger that they are not necessarily related to the reason the person attended the event in the first place and therefore may again lead to subjective evaluation or rationalization. However, not all the questions can be answered immediately. Evaluation therefore must be carried out in at least two stages: immediately after the event and some time later. Combining the first set of questions with the last set can lead to effective evaluation.

Before looking at methods it is worth remembering that the Investors in People indicators require evaluation to be carried out at three levels: organizational, team and individual. In very small organizations it may be difficult to separate the team and organizational levels.

So how do you do it?

At the end of the event

The first opportunity for evaluation is at the end of the event, ideally before leaving, and the trainer or facilitator of the event therefore manages this process. Most facilitators, whether they are in-house or external, have some kind of evaluation such as course critiques or reaction sheets, more commonly referred to as 'happy sheets'. They are a type of evaluation and if constructed carefully can give an immediate reaction as to whether the participant *thinks* the objectives have been met.

It is also possible to encourage people to review the event by including questions about what they have learnt, as illustrated in the example of a course critique included in Figure 9.2. Incidentally, 'happy sheets' can also be used to evaluate the various services that go into supporting an activity, such as catering and administration, and therefore can provide managers with additional useful information to refine further the training and development provided.

Going through the above process can, therefore, contribute to evaluation evidence mainly at organizational level but may contribute at individual and team level too.

Post-event debriefs – immediately after

It is almost impossible for some kind of debrief not to take place. It is rare for a person to return from an event without someone (ideally the line manager) asking the questions, 'How did it go?', 'Was it helpful?' or perhaps, 'Did you enjoy it?' To make this more meaningful as an exercise in evaluation, questions such as the following need to be asked:

- 'Was the event successful in meeting the objectives we agreed before the event?'
- 'How will you use the skills or apply the knowledge that you gained?'
- 'Do you now *think* you can do what we hoped you would be able to do, which we discussed before you went on the event?'

- 'When should we review how you are *using* the skills and knowledge?'

Part B of the evaluation form shown in Appendix 3 could be used at this stage in the evaluation process.

Post-event debriefs – after a while

It is amazing that many organizations and their managers miss this stage in evaluation. When asked how their manager knows whether the skills learnt on the training or developmental event are being used, many people simply don't know. Many managers simply *assume* that the skills will be used; others see that they are being used but don't acknowledge it with their people. In one case the manager, a Head of Department in a school, did it secretly by watching the teacher's performance through a crack in the door! How long after an event it is worth reviewing the application of skills and/or knowledge depends on the complexity of the training and development. If a group of people attended an event, a post-event debriefing may contribute to evaluation at the team as well as the individual level.

The third part of the form shown in Appendix 3 could be used for this stage in the evaluation process.

Via the appraisal or training/development review process

As discussed in Chapter 6, in order to deliver the required outcomes needed to become an Investor in People an organization has to have a process to identify development needs. This process, whether it is an appraisal process or something else, should offer an opportunity for evaluation. Training and/or development objectives will have been agreed at the previous review; they should be discussed, along with how the activity has impacted on performance, before agreeing new objectives.

This is also the start of gathering information about the benefits of developmental activity.

Learning logs

Some organizations have encouraged individuals to keep learning logs. Although they may be seen as a bureaucratic chore, they can be very useful in a number of ways.

EVALUATION OF INVESTORS IN PEOPLE WORKSHOP
Line Manager's Role
Date:
Please indicate how satisfied you were against each question by ticking:
1 Very satisfied   2 Satisfied   3 Unsatisfied   4 Very unsatisfied

1. How successful was the workshop in meeting its aim and objectives?

	1	2	3	4
Aim	☐	☐	☐	☐
Objective (a)	☐	☐	☐	☐
Objective (b)	☐	☐	☐	☐
Objective (c)	☐	☐	☐	☐
Objective (d)	☐	☐	☐	☐
Objective (e)	☐	☐	☐	☐

Comments

	1	2	3	4
2. How helpful was the workshop in meeting your objectives?	☐	☐	☐	☐

Was the length of the workshop: Too long ☐
About right ☐
Too short? ☐

Comments

3. Can you make any suggestions to improve the workshop?

4. What were the three most important points you learnt during the workshop?

5. Are there any other Investors in People topics you would like to see addressed in future workshops?

Please indicate how you felt about:	1	2	3	4
Facilitator's presentation	☐	☐	☐	☐
Quality of handouts	☐	☐	☐	☐

Thank you.

Figure 9.2 *Example of a course critique or reaction sheet*

They come in various forms and often link to personal/individual development plans. Some may keep them as a record that will contribute to their Continuous Professional Development (CPD), which many professional bodies require their members to demonstrate.

Learning logs are useful in that they enable the individual to review what has been learnt from training and/or developmental actions in a systematic way. Quite often, people (and we include ourselves here) return from training or developmental activities full of good intentions of reviewing the notes and handouts that have been given and of implementing some of the ideas that were suggested or thoughts that were triggered by the event. The good intentions often disappear under the volume of work that meets you on your return. The discipline of having a structured method of reviewing what was learnt and entering it in a learning log is a useful one to develop.

Unless there is a CPD requirement, keeping learning logs needs a discipline that is largely self-imposed. Those organizations that tried to introduce learning logs as a policy often found that a large number of people did not complete them because they can be time-consuming, especially if not done on a regular basis. It is therefore better for organizations, through managers, to sell the concept and the benefits rather than try to impose it.

Where learning logs are kept they can contribute, at the individual level, to evaluation of what was learnt and how it has been applied.

Achievement of qualifications, including NVQs

This is probably the most straightforward form of evaluation. When the outcome of training and development is the achievement of a qualification, this indicates that the objectives of the activity have been met and therefore contributes to the evaluation of the effectiveness of the training.

Assessment of competence against National Standards through the NVQ process is another form of evaluation. However, it is also important, when using NVQ assessments to illustrate evaluation, to be able to demonstrate what has been *learnt* and how it has affected performance. In some cases the achievement of an NVQ may be merely confirming what the person has been able to do for some time and little learning may have taken place. While the achievement of the NVQ may have a motivational payback, especially if that person has never before had a piece of paper that says they are competent, the impact on performance may be marginal.

Sharing or cascading learning

In order to manage training budgets effectively, instead of sending a number of people on training events many organizations ask those who do attend to present a summary of the event to colleagues. There are a number of disadvantages to this method of training, especially if the 'presenter' is not trained in presentational skills. We have, however, seen this approach used effectively and it can offer managers the chance to monitor what *has* been learnt and can therefore contribute to the evaluation of training and development.

Evaluation and project management

A large number of organizations will at some stage involve their staff in project work. For some, such as construction and civil engineering companies, property consultants, etc, their whole business is made up of projects. For example, in the Health and Safety Laboratory at Sheffield, part of the Health and Safety Executive, a large amount of their work is project-based, either investigating the causes of accidents at work or carrying out research on behalf of clients who wish to prevent the accidents in the first place.

To have a successful project there must be a project plan and part of that plan is likely to involve initial research at the very least. Experts may well be brought in to offer advice and guidance, but throughout the project there will be a great deal of *learning*, which may or may not be caught in the end-of-project report. It is not always easy to capture this type of learning but if it is planned into the project at an early stage it can contribute to effective evaluation.

Evaluation and continuous improvement

In a similar way, learning through continuous improvement projects or groups may contribute to evaluation. Again, it may not always have been planned to identify such learning but with a little thought at the planning stage it should be possible to capture sufficient information about increases in knowledge and/or skills. Sometimes it is difficult to separate the 'learning' from other outcomes, especially if the improvement focused on improved systems or processes, in which case some aspects of learning will merely be implied.

Avoiding the paper chase

There is often a concern regarding the potential bureaucracy of Investors in People and, without care, evaluation in particular can become very bureaucratic. It is therefore important to examine the processes that already exist and see if they can be used to help with evaluation.

A lot of the most essential processes mentioned above have already been mentioned earlier in this book and, for those organizations working towards Investors in People, will probably already exist or will have been introduced to satisfy earlier criteria. With just a little tweaking they can be used for evaluative purposes. We are always loath to add more paperwork, but the process of debriefing is easy to forget if it is not part of the culture or if managers are not naturally people managers. It is therefore advisable, especially in the early stages, to have a paper system (such as the form in Appendix 3) that prompts managers to carry out these debriefs. It also enables organizations to 'audit' the post-training activity until debriefing becomes embedded in and therefore part of the culture, when the paperwork could become redundant.

Evaluating development

In Chapter 6 we examined methods of development. Because development may be less tangible than training, evaluation is not always that easy, as the following illustration shows. During the course of an Investors in People assessment, one of us interviewed a person who, he had been informed, had been 'developed'. When the person was asked how she had learnt the job she was doing she said she had 'picked it up'. It was only after a great deal of probing that the interviewee remembered that she had 'picked it up' through a well-structured development programme with a number of distinct activities that formed the programme. This therefore prompts the question, 'How do you evaluate development?'

There could be a temptation to evaluate every single developmental activity (although it is evident that many organizations are not so tempted!). In Chapter 6 we floated the idea of clustering developmental activities into 'programmes' or developmental projects. Although the three-stage form in Appendix 3 could be used as a pre-programme briefing, it would be simpler to use the appraisal or review process as the vehicle for setting aims and objectives and reviewing them. For those organizations that encourage the use of personal development plans, they would be the vehicle for evaluating effectiveness.

Agreeing and recording aims and objectives and evaluating the 'development programme' is therefore the simple and unbureaucratic method of evaluating 'development'. It may also avoid people who have been developed saying that they merely 'picked it up'.

Evaluating the impact of training and development

Many organizations find this is difficult to do. The first question to ask is, 'Did the training and/or development have the planned effect?' This implies, of course, that there was a planned, desired effect. As we have often reiterated, effective evaluation does not mean scratching heads and trying to work out what effect the training contribution has had after the event. Effective evaluation is checking actual outcomes against planned outcomes. There will of course be 'by-products', those unintended outcomes (hopefully beneficial!) and these should also be acknowledged, but the simplest approach to evaluation is based on having 'SMART/SUMATRA' objectives at the planning stage (see Chapter 6).

This is as relevant at the organizational level as it is at the team and individual level. It is not as simple at the organizational level, especially in larger organizations. It often means having some system for collating information gathered at team and individual levels. This may imply a layer of bureaucracy but it does not need to. In the early chapters of this book we described how organizations used a meetings structure to inform employees. The same structure can be used to pass information back up to the top about the effectiveness and benefits of training and development.

Some organizations use written processes to gather such information, with formal procedures or written reviews of training and
development presented to senior management meetings. Whatever
method is chosen it is important that it works; if it doesn't – change
it.

This then links to the evaluation of systems. As Investors in
People is aligned to total quality and therefore continuous improvement, it is important that the effectiveness of the training and
development systems and processes is reviewed too. This is especially important when they are new.

Did we get value for money?

In Chapter 4 the need to know the costs and benefits of training is
seen as part of the role of senior managers. The question of getting
value for money is often a difficult one for many senior managers
to answer. Perhaps the question should be reworded – 'Did you
get the *planned* value for money?'

Throughout this book we have referred to the need to link
training and development to the needs of the organization and the
need to set SMART objectives. Part of this SMARTness should
include the anticipated return on the investment of time and money
in delivering the training and development.

It really comes back to what the business objective was. For
example, was the training and development and subsequent
increased application of skills and/or knowledge supposed to lead
to an increase in production? To save time? To improve service in
order to get repeat business?

All of these can be measured and given an anticipated monetary
value, as can the cost of the training and development in terms of
time and/or money spent. After a period of time following the
training, a comparison of the cost of the training against the actual
improvements in terms of increased production, time saved, etc
can give you a simple cost–benefit analysis which shows whether
value for money was achieved.

Many readers will now be saying that it's not as simple as that!
It's not possible to measure the impact of some training in those
terms. They will probably cite management training as an example.

But why are managers trained and/or developed? To be less efficient? If they are more efficient will they not:

- Carry out their job in less time?
- Or juggle more balls at the same time?
- Or manage their time more efficiently?
- Or get more efficiency from their people?

Again, all these things could be measured in some way and a value placed on the improvements. This of course could become quite complex and it is at this point that a judgement has to be made whether value for money is being achieved from carrying out the cost–benefit analysis itself. We do believe that while the cost–benefit analysis may not satisfy the purists, if the measures are kept fairly simple it would give a rough idea of value for money. Without trying to establish value for money, how do you know the money is not being wasted?

If all else fails, ask yourself the simple question: 'If this was my money, would I still spend it on the training and development?' If the answer is yes, then ask yourself, why? The answer to the second question will go some way to proving whether you are getting value for money. A handy checklist, usable at the individual, team and organizational level, is shown in Figure 9.3.

Self-Audit

- [ ] *What are you trying to achieve?*
- [ ] *Why are you trying to achieve it?*
- [ ] *How are you trying to achieve it?*
- [ ] *Why are you doing it that way?*
- [ ] *Is it the best way of doing it?*
- [ ] *Is it effective?*
- [ ] *How do you check its effectiveness?*
- [ ] *What do you do as a result of the check?*

Figure 9.3 *An evaluation checklist*

What do managers need to do?

- Immediately after returning from an event, check what was learnt and whether the participant thinks the objectives agreed before the event were met.
- After an appropriate time, discuss with the participant whether the skills and knowledge are being used and whether they are able to achieve what was expected prior to the event taking place.
- During appraisals or reviews, check that previously set learning objectives have been met.
- Try to capture information about what has been learnt through project work or continuous improvement activity.
- Keep a simple record of benefits to the person, team or organization so that it can be passed on to senior managers or whoever is responsible for collating such information at the organizational level.

Summary

This chapter has examined the evaluation of training in the context of Investors in People. It has examined a variety of methods and useful but simple approaches. It has described the roles that managers at all levels should have in the evaluation process and how they can contribute to gathering information on behalf of the organization as whole, including whether value for money is being achieved.

CHAPTER 10

The Manager's Role in Retaining Investor in People Status

With more than 24,250 organizations recognized who will all face a post-recognition review at least every three years, it is necessary to explore the manager's role in retaining the recognition as an Investor in People.

This chapter looks at some of the pitfalls, 'traps' and obstacles we have met while working with organizations which are approaching reassessment, and offers some thoughts as to how managers can help avoid or overcome them.

Post-recognition euphoria

Clearly, when an organization is recognized as an Investor in People it is time for celebration. The level of euphoria will be related to the amount of effort put into preparing the organization for assessment. We have often referred to recognition as being a 'milestone on a journey'. For organizations that have used the Investors in People principles for a long time, the effort may well not have been as great as for those that have introduced them more recently.

It is those organizations for which the first major milestone *is* recognition that are the most vulnerable to letting systems slip into disuse and thus the required outcomes may not be delivered. In these organizations people will have worked hard to achieve the Standard. There will be a 'plateau' period directly after recognition. It is possible that this period may become extended. This should not happen where systems are embedded, but it does.

Why do processes fall into disuse?

The reasons for this are many and varied. Sometimes, quite simply, processes are not as embedded as they should be, or as senior staff think they are. By checking that the processes are delivering the required outcomes, assessors are trying to ensure that they are embedded, especially new ones. This generally means that they have been used twice and reviewed and improved. When interviewing, assessors will try to judge whether the people agree that processes have become embedded. They will also wish to ascertain if the processes would actually be missed if for any reason they fell into disuse.

As we have suggested throughout this book, the required outcomes rely on processes and processes rely on managers and their commitment to making them work. Clearly the responsibility to *continue* the use of the processes also falls back on to managers. Quite often, when processes have fallen into disuse, it is because they are too complex and/or time-consuming. Managers have found them to be a chore – a bolt-on activity, not part of 'normal' work – and have therefore stopped using them. Unless there are procedures in place to pick this up it may not be noticed until reassessment approaches.

Gaining recognition through linking Investors in People to a major in-house programme

Many organizations have coupled major initiatives with their approach to Investors in People, such as a customer care programme or a culture change perhaps linked to multi-skilling. It makes a lot of sense and it may well make it easier to demonstrate improvements through training and development, especially if the organization was starting from a low baseline. However, success with these programmes may also lead to a false sense of security and things may again plateau. Even if the programme continues it is unlikely that previously impressive results will keep appearing. It is therefore essential for managers to be aware of this possibility and to look for ways of seeking further improvements. At the same time, they should make people aware that improvements may not be on the same *scale* as before, but are just as important.

Continuous improvement

We have found that organizations that have approached Investors in People from a total quality or continuous improvement angle are, in the main, more aware of the pitfalls. They are also less likely to allow systems to slip. The ethos of continual review and looking for a better way of doing things means that complex systems would be reviewed and simplified. They will be continuously keeping abreast of the latest trends and ideas and assessing their relevance to their own organizations.

They will not assume anything, as they are also likely to have quality monitoring and evaluation procedures that show if and when processes are falling into disuse. Action would then be taken to investigate why this was happening or perhaps just to remind people to take appropriate action. Doing this will avoid the last minute (or months') panic when it is realized that the date for reassessment is fast approaching.

Many organizations realize that they cannot sit back following recognition. One organization drew up a strategy to take the following actions:

1. Continue to canvas employee opinion by repeating a diagnostic or staff attitude survey annually.
2. Involve their managers through a process of self-assessment against the Investors in People indicators and evidence requirements.

3. Through the above process they intend risk-banding any activity, or lack of it, in line with their normal quality policy. Following the risk-banding, action would take place as follows:
   Red: High risk   Requires urgent action
   Amber: Low risk   Requires action
   Green: No risk   Some minor action may be required.
4. Keeping a development scorecard. This involved recording factual information about the number of people trained and developed each month, comparing it with previous years, and recording trainee satisfaction.
5. They are also planning to introduce the management NVQs.

It is interesting to compare what has been written in this book with what Deming, one of the total quality gurus, called his '14 points' (Walton, 1989); these are reproduced below:

1. Create constancy of purpose for the improvement of product and service.
2. Adopt the new philosophy for the new economic age with management learning what their responsibilities are, and by assuming leadership.
3. Cease dependence on mass inspection to achieve quality by building quality into the product.
4. End the practice of awarding business on price tag alone.
5. Improve constantly and forever the system of production and service.
6. Institute training and retraining.
7. Institute leadership with the aim of supervising people to help them do a better job.
8. Drive out fear so that everyone can work effectively together for the organization.
9. Break down barriers between departments.
10. Eliminate slogans, exhortations and targets for the workforce.
11. Eliminate numerical quotas.
12. Remove barriers to pride of workmanship.
13. Institute a vigorous programme of education and a self-improvement programme.
14. Put everyone in the company to work to accomplish the transformation.

While not all are directly related to the Investors in People issues we have referred to throughout this book, there are certainly a number of overlaps, especially those concerned with continuous improvement through management, leadership, communication and of course training and development. Training and development and *learning* are at the heart of continuous improvement and therefore at the heart of total quality.

Evaluating learning through continuous improvement

As organizations move away from formal training and into learning through continuous improvement, the learning becomes less tangible. It therefore becomes more difficult to evaluate the impact of the learning as distinct from the *improvement, which* may often be to do with systems and processes. Some may question whether there is a need to distinguish the learning in this way: to retain Investors in People status it may be necessary in the absence of more traditional and tangible training activity. In Chapter 9 we referred to learning logs and how we found that some people keep them to record what they have learnt and how the learning may be applied. Encouraging people to do this could be a way of satisfying an assessor. It will also fulfil CPD requirements for those who need to.

Senior managers and *continued* commitment

The first thing for senior managers to remember to recognize is that retaining Investors in People status needs effort too. The good practice concerning the *demonstration* of their commitment mentioned in Chapter 4 should be continued, but other senior manager actions are also required. If little or nothing more is done by senior managers it will reinforce in the minds of the cynics that they were only committed to getting the badge and not to the principles and philosophy of Investors in People.

What do senior managers need to do?

The continued use of systems and processes should identify the successes brought about through training and development. It should become part of the culture of the organization that senior managers, especially, publicly acknowledge the part that training and development have played in business success and that they will therefore *continue* to be committed to them. . . because it pays to do so.

They should encourage the philosophy of continuous improvement being extended to improving the training and development itself and the processes and systems that underpin it. Standing still is not good enough.

Summary

This chapter has examined the manager's role in retaining Investors in People status and related it to the concept of total quality and the quest for continuous improvement. It has pointed out a number of the pitfalls and made suggestions as to how to avoid them. Finally, it has reminded senior managers of the need to *continue* to be committed to developing their people and how this can be demonstrated.

The Investors in People Standard

Principles	Indicators	Evidence requirement
Commitment An Investor in People is fully committed to developing its people in order to achieve its aims and objectives	**1** The organisation is committed to supporting the development of its people	Top management can describe strategies that they have put in place to support the development of people in order to improve the organisation's performance Managers can describe specific actions that they have taken and are currently taking to support the development of people People can confirm that the specific strategies and actions described by top management and managers take place People believe the organisation is genuinely committed to supporting their development

Principles	Indicators	Evidence requirement
	2 People are encouraged to improve their own and other people's performance	People can give examples of how they have been encouraged to improve their own performance People can give examples of how they have been encouraged to improve other people's performance
	3 People believe their contribution to the organisation is recognised	People can describe how their contribution to the organisation is recognised People believe that their contribution to the organisation is recognised People receive appropriate and constructive feedback on a timely and regular basis
	4 The organisation is committed to ensuring equality of opportunity in the development of its people	Top management can describe strategies that they have put in place to ensure equality of opportunity in the development of people Managers can describe specific actions that they have taken and are currently taking to ensure equality of opportunity in the development of people People confirm that the specific strategies and actions described by top management and managers take place and recognise the needs of different groups People believe the organisation is genuinely committed to ensuring equality of opportunity in the development of people

Principles	Indicators	Evidence requirement
Planning An Investor in People is clear about its aims and its objectives and what its people need to do to achieve them	5 The organisation has a plan with clear aims and objectives which are understood by everyone	The organisation has a plan with clear aims and objectives People can consistently explain the aims and objectives of the organisation at a level appropriate to their role Representative groups are consulted about the organisation's aims and objectives
	6 The development of people is in line with the organisation's aims and objectives	The organisation has clear priorities which link the development of people to its aims and objectives at organisation, team and individual level People clearly understand what their development activities should achieve, both for them and the organisation
	7 People understand how they contribute to achieving the organisation's aims and objectives	People can explain how they contribute to achieving the organisation's aims and objectives
Action An Investor in People develops its people effectively in order to improve its performance	8 Managers are effective in supporting the development of people	The organisation makes sure that managers have the knowledge and skills they need to develop their people Managers at all levels understand what they need to do to support the development of people People understand what their manager should be doing to support their development

Principles	Indicators	Evidence requirement
		Managers at all levels can give examples of actions that they have taken and are currently taking to support the development of people
		People can describe how their managers are effective in supporting their development
	9 People learn and develop effectively	People who are new to the organisation, and those new to a job, can confirm that they have received an effective induction
		The organisation can show that people learn and develop effectively
		People understand why they have undertaken development activities and what they are expected to do as a result
		People can give examples of what they have learnt (knowledge, skills and attitude) from development activities
		Development is linked to relevant external qualifications or standards (or both), where appropriate
Evaluation An Investor in People understands the impact of its investment in people on its performance	10 The development of people improves the performance of the organisation, teams and individuals	The organisation can show that the development of people has improved the performance of the organisation, teams and individuals

Principles	Indicators	Evidence requirement
	11 People understand the impact of the development of people on the performance of the organisation, teams and individuals	Top management understands the overall costs and benefits of the development of people and its impact on performance People can explain the impact of their development on their performance, and the performance of their team and the organisation as a whole
	12 The organisation gets better at developing its people	People can give examples of relevant and timely improvements that have been made to development activities

The Standard © Investors in People UK.

Sources of Help

This is a 'Who's who' of the various sources of help available to assist organizations through the process.

As addresses, telephone numbers and to some extent even Web site addresses can soon become out of date, it does not give full details of all the sources. It does not attempt to list all sources but merely points to the key players who in turn may have their own sources to which they redirect anyone who wants to know more.

Investors in People UK

Investors in People UK was established in July 1993 as a private company limited by guarantee. It opened for business on 1 October 1993. Originally based in Sheffield, it moved to premises at 7–10 Chandos Street, London W1G 9DQ in April 1994. Investors in People has a Web site: http://www.investorsinpeople.co.uk

The role of Investors in People UK is:

- to guard, direct and take the lead on the development of the Investors in People National Standard, in the UK and internationally;
- to define the assessment process in outline;
- national promotion and support;
- national quality assurance;

- assessment and recognition of national organizations and originally TECs/LECs and now local Learning and Skills Councils;
- promotion of the standard internationally.

Investors in People UK works in close consultation with all its partners.

The local delivery organizations

Learning & Skills Councils and Business Links

In England the delivery network consists of the Local Learning and Skills Councils (LLSCs) and the Business Links.

The Learning and Skills Council (LSC) and the network of 47 LLSCs became operational in April 2001. Their role is to fund further education and take forward government funded training and workforce development in England, with a budget of some £5 billion. The LLSCs succeed the Training and Enterprise Councils (TECs), which spent £1 billion on training, and the Further Education Funding Council, which spent over £3 billion on further education. The enterprise role of TECs is to be taken forward by the DTI's Small Business Service.

Raising standards and delivering high quality training, including national learning targets, will be central to the success of the LSC, which will also include a new inspection system, based on existing expertise with work-based training, to help drive up quality. Information about the LSC and the LLSCs can be found on the DfEE Web site: www.dfes.gov.uk/post16/

In relation to Investors in People the LLSCs will generally deal with all public and voluntary sector organizations and all large private sector organizations, ie those employing more than 250 people. Private sector organizations employing less than 250 employees will be dealt with by Business Links.

Information about the Small Business Service can be found on www.businessadviceonline.org

Investors in People Scotland

Investors in People Scotland is a company limited by guarantee established to carry out assessments and arrange the recognition of Scottish organizations on behalf of Local Enterprise Companies, the Scottish counterparts of LLSCs. They are based in Edinburgh.

Scotland – Local Enterprise Companies (LECs)

LECs were set up at about the same time as TECs but they have a wider remit, as they not only took over the delivery of products and services such as youth and adult training, but also embraced the role of the Scottish Development Agency and the Highlands and Islands Development Agency.

LECs are private companies limited by guarantee who are contracted to either Scottish Enterprise or Highlands and Islands Enterprise. There are 22 LECs although some counts might show 23, as one straddles the border between Scottish Enterprise and Highlands and Islands Enterprise and is often counted twice.

Assessment and recognition is carried out by Investors in People Scotland so the role of the LECs is to carry out the same work as TECs minus assessment and recognition. They too use outsiders to deliver various stages of Investors in People.

The phone numbers and addresses of LECs can be found in local telephone directories or you could access information via the Investors in People UK Web site at www.investorsinpeople.co.uk/Services/scot1.htm

Education and Learning Wales (ELWa)

The National Council for Education and Training for Wales and the Higher Education Funding Council for Wales are responsible for all post-16 education and training in Wales. Together these organizations are known as ELWa, Education and Learning Wales.

Among other tasks ELWa is responsible for the delivery of Investors in People in Wales. More information is available from their Web site at www.elwa.org.uk

Northern Ireland – Training and Employment Agency (T&EA)

The T&EA was established as an agency of the Northern Ireland Civil Service in 1990 and is now part of the Department of Higher & Further Education, Training and Employment. It carries out a role similar to that of the Department for Education and

Employment in England and Wales. One of its divisions has a particular remit to support business and it is under this requirement that Investors in People sits.

The Agency has broadly the same role as the LLSCs in delivering Investors in People. However, the financial support offered by the T&EA is through the Agency's Company Development Programme and the consultants who deliver it.

Their Web site can also be accessed via the Investors in People UK site at www.investorsinpeople.co.uk/Services/nireland.htm

National Training Organizations (NTOs)

The NTO National Council was founded in October 1997 to represent and support the new network of NTOs that was launched in May 1998. Its predecessor organization, NCITO, represented ITOs and other related bodies from the 1980s.

The launch of the NTO network marked a major rationalization of the previous infrastructure, replacing the ITOs, Lead Bodies and Occupational Standards Councils (OSCs) that had been in existence from the 1980s, with a single NTO for each industry or occupational sector. In addition to taking over many of their activities, NTOs have a far wider strategic remit defined by government.

Every sector has its own NTO. Seventy-five NTOs have been recognized by the government to date, each representing an individual industry (such as construction or hospitality), or occupation that affects all sectors (such as information technology or management). NTOs cover the whole of the UK. They are owned and supported by employers and serve organizations of every size.

NTOs' role is to bring together employers, government and the world of education and training to define and take forward a focused agenda for skills. Their work ranges from assisting in the development and implementation of national and regional policies on learning and skills, to assessing the skills needs and impact of their sector, and developing practical solutions to training problems on behalf of their industries. NTOs have a key role with regard to Investors in People – for example, joint projects, producing practical guides, case studies and other supportive sector-specific material.

The origins of NTOs date back to the mid-1960s, when the then government made the first moves towards a structure of employer representation. A network of Industry Training Boards (ITBs) was established. ITBs were given the power to raise a levy to be used to further vocational education and training from companies within their defined sectors.

During the 1980s most ITBs were wound up and ITOs were developed. By the mid-1990s – and with the expansion of the NVQ/SVQ system – the plethora of organizations, ie ITOs, Lead Bodies, and Occupational Standards Councils had become extremely confusing for business people. All were provided with a detailed prospectus containing new criteria and were invited to apply for recognition as NTOs – National Training Organizations.

One of the authors works for the National Training Organization for Higher Education (HESDA, see below). Their first aim is 'to promote strategically planned, continuing and coherent staff development and training provision across universities and colleges in the United Kingdom'.

For further information about NTOs contact The NTO National Council, 10 Amos Road, Meadow Court, Sheffield S9 1BX, Tel: (0114) 261 9926, Web site: http://www.nto-nc.org/

The Higher Education Staff Development Agency (HESDA)

HESDA, formerly known as UCoSDA, was created in 1989. It is one of the agencies of the Committee of Vice Chancellors and Principals and was recognized as the National Training Organization for higher education (THETO) in November 1997.

HESDA seeks to provide advice, support and resources to its member universities and colleges in the planning, organization, provision and evaluation of continuing professional/vocational development for all personnel in the higher education sector.

It currently employs an approved Investors in People assessor – one of the authors of this book. The HESDA philosophy captures some of the central themes of this book and is summarized as follows:

Investment in the personal, professional and vocational development of all staff employed by universities and colleges is fundamental:

(a) to the successful achievement of organizational goals and
(b) to the motivation and continuing capacity of individual staff members to support that achievement.

HESDA has produced a number of briefing papers and other publications on Investors in People and related issues and can be contacted at: Ingram House, 65 Wilkinson Street, The University of Sheffield, Sheffield S10 2GJ, Tel: 0114 282 4211, Fax: 0114 272 8705, Web site: www.hesda.org.uk

Management Charter Initiative (MCI)

For information on the Management Standards or the booklets *Managing Business Success* and *The Good Managers Guide* contact The Management Standards Unit, Russell Square House, 10–12 Russell Square, London WC1B 5BZ, Tel: 020 7872 9000, Web site: www.management-charter-initiative.org.uk

Qualifications and Curriculum Authority

Information about NVQs can be obtained from the QCA at 83 Piccadilly, London W1J 8QA, Tel: 020 7509 555, Web site: www.qca.org.uk

Consultants and consultancy organizations

Feelings about using consultants differ considerably from one organization (or person) to another but this section is included for those who may wish to consider the use of consultants. This section does not intend to debate the relative merits of using them; the arguments are well rehearsed elsewhere. However, because historically the resources within TECs have been limited, they and LECs have encouraged the use of outside help to deliver the various stages of Investors in People. As in-house expertise grew, and budgets were reduced, some TECs in particular used their own staff to offer assistance. The changes to the assessment process also led to less reliance on consultants, particularly for smaller organizations. With the advent of Learning and Skills Councils and the Small Business Service, we will have to wait and see if there is sufficient in-house resource or whether there may be a resurgence in demand for help from external sources.

Investors in People UK developed a quality assurance (QA) process for consultants and advisers who work with organizations on Investors in People. The process covers roles such as selling, diagnosing and developing and implementing action plans, which includes management training and development. The QA process is managed by Regional Quality Centres (see Taylor and Thackwray, 2001a) throughout the UK and approved by Investors in People UK.

At the moment the QA registration process for potential advisers involves sitting a written multi-choice examination followed by a situational interview in front of an interview panel.

Investors in People UK took an interest in this subject as the credibility of the process of becoming an Investor in People was being affected by advice and guidance being given that was not as good as it should have been. Although the process for consultants and advisors new to Investors in People will change during 2001 there will still be a QA process that will use the new Investors in People practitioner competencies as a basis plus an interview.

How consultants can help
Provided you get the right consultant they can help in a number of ways. They may help you secure some financial support. They should have experience of carrying out certain tasks and can therefore help you avoid reinventing wheels.

They *should* know what an assessor expects of you but ensure that you are not merely introducing things for an assessor but are doing them for sound business reasons too. In most cases the needs of the assessor will coincide with your needs but you need to challenge the consultant constantly if you feel you are being asked to do something from which you will gain no business benefits.

They should have experience or an understanding of related models such as the ISO 9000 series, the Business Excellence Model, Ofsted, Lexcel and other quality models and processes and how they complement Investors in People. Again this will avoid reinventing wheels.

Other organizations

The help offered by peers who have been recognized and perhaps maintained their recognition may prove valuable. The first organizations to be recognized and subsequently re-recognized were inundated by callers who wanted to know how they did it; some of them may well have wondered why they got involved. However, now there are a lot more people to offer this kind of guidance.

Most TECs and LECs have invited representatives from recognized organizations to speak at local events so you may well find out about them then. It is likely that the LLSCs will continue this practice. If not, or if you need to identify a specific type of organization, your LLSC/SBS/LEC will be able to help identify and put you in touch with someone who can help.

Overseas sources of help

Sources of help overseas is a little more complex. Investors in People UK has developed strategic partnerships to pilot Investors in People. In the first overseas country to launch, Australia, the strategic Partner is NCSI (Nata Certification Services International), an existing organization. In Finland the partner is the University of Helsinki while in the Netherlands a new body has been established – Investors in People Nederland.

At the same time consultancies that can assist organizations are emerging as sources of advice, such as the PerSyst ECPM Consultancy in the Netherlands who found a case study for us which we used in another of our books (Taylor and Thackwray, 2001a). Visit the Investors in People UK Web site (see above) to discover who the strategic partner for each country is.

Investors in People material, videos, etc

Finally, there is a wealth of material available to help you work through the process. In addition to local material there is a lot of nationally available material produced by Investors in People UK (a catalogue is available and accessible via the Investors in People UK Web site – see above). There are also a lot of articles in management and training magazines and books either being written or already in existence to help you gain an understanding of what Investors in People is and how it can promote organizational development. This book and our earlier ones (Taylor and Thackwray, 2001a and b) are all examples!

Sample Evaluation Sheet

Evaluation of training and development effectiveness

Name: _____

Section/Department: _____

Part A. Prior to the training or development action

1. Proposed training/development activity _____

2. Details, eg, dates, locations, cost _____

   _____

   _____

3. The business objective the proposed activity will help to achieve

   _____

   _____

   _____

4. The skills and/or knowledge that will be learnt as a result of the activity

   _____

   _____

5. How the new skills and/or knowledge will be applied after the activity

_____

_____

6. Line manager's comments, ie, expectations in terms of targets or standards _____

_____

_____

Signatures _____ Participant _____ date _____

_____ Line manager _____ date _____

Part B. Immediately after the training and/or developmental activity

1. Did the participant attend   yes/no (if no give reason)

_____

_____

2. To what extent has this activity met the agreed training and/or development need?

Please circle   Not at all   1   2   3   4   Totally

Comments

_____

_____

3. How will the learning be applied?

_____

_____

_____

4. What help/support is needed to put the learning into practice?

_____

_____

_____

5. To what extent did the activity represent:

(a) Value for money

Please circle   Not at all   1   2   3   4   Totally

(a) An acceptable standard of delivery

Please circle   Not at all   1   2   3   4   Totally

Comments

_____

_____

6. Agreed date to review

Signatures _____ Participant _____date _____

_____ Line manager _____date _____

Part C. Review to monitor impact on performance

1. How has the learning been applied since the activity?

_____

_____

2. To what extent have the agreed objectives/targets or standards been met?

Please circle   Not at all   1   2   3   4   Totally

Comments

_____

_____

3. If learning has not been applied please state why

_____

_____

4. What further action or review is required?

Signatures _____ Participant _____date _____

_____ Line manager _____date _____

References

Hammer, M and Champy, J (1993) *Re-engineering the Corporation – A manifesto for business revolution,* Nicholas Brearley, London

Institute of Management and UMIST (2001) *Quality of Working Life,* Institute of Management and UMIST, Manchester

New Zealand Universities Academic Audit Unit (1995) *Audit Manual: Handbook for institutions and members of audit panels,* New Zealand Universities Academic Audit Unit, Wellington

Peters, T and Waterman, R (1982) *In Search of Excellence,* Harper &Row, New York

Taylor, P and Thackwray, R (2001a) *Investors in People Explained,* 4th edn, Kogan Page, London

Taylor, P and Thackwray, R (2001b) *Investors in People Maintained,* 2nd edn, Kogan Page, London

Walton, M (1989) *The Deming Management Method,* Mercury, London

Index